Writing the Ancestral River

Writing the Ancestral River

A biography of the Kowie

Jacklyn Cock

WITS UNIVERSITY PRESS

Published in South Africa by:

Wits University Press
1 Jan Smuts Avenue
Johannesburg, 2001
www.witspress.co.za

Copyright © Jacklyn Cock 2018
Published edition © Wits University Press 2018

Photographs © Copyright holders 2018
Poems © Copyright holders 2018, used with permission

Cover images:
Top: Map of the country between the Kowie and the Chalumna rivers, Caesar C. Henkel, 1876. University of Cape Town Libraries, Historical Map Collection.
Bottom: 'Kowie, looking seaward', lithograph by F. Jones from painting by Thomas Bowler, hand coloured. Cory Library/Africa Media Online.

First published 2018

http://dx.doi.org.10.18772/12018031876

978-1-77614-187-6 (Print)
978-1-77614-188-3 (Web PDF)
978-1-77614-189-0 (EPUB)

All rights reserved. No part of this publication may be reproduced, stored in a retrieval system, or transmitted in any form or by any means, electronic, mechanical, photocopying, recording or otherwise, without the written permission of the publisher, except in accordance with the provisions of the Copyright Act, Act 98 of 1978.

All images remain the property of the copyright holders. The publishers gratefully acknowledge the publishers, institutions and individuals referenced in the captions for the use of images. Every effort has been made to locate the original copyright holders of the images reproduced here; please contact Wits University Press in case of any omissions or errors

Project manager: Hazel Cuthbertson
Copy editor: Russell Martin
Proofreader: Lisa Compton
Indexer: Tessa Botha
Cover design: Peter Bosman, Guineafolio
Typesetter: Newgen

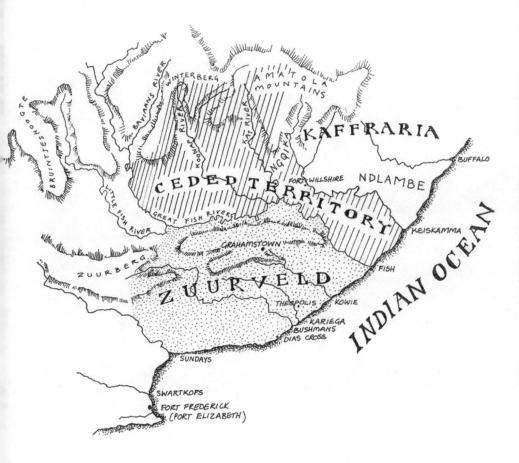

The Kowie River runs through the centre of what was once called the 'Zuurveld', originally defined in the early 1800s as the area between the Bushmans River in the west and the Fish River in the east. The boundary was later extended further west to the Sundays River (Map by Hazel Crampton, from *The Sunburnt Queen*, Jacana, 2004).

Contents

Acknowledgements

This book draws heavily on the published work of many historians with far more knowledge and insight than I possess. I have learnt a great deal particularly from Tim Keegan, Basil Le Cordeur, Jeff Peires, Clifton Crais and especially Julie Wells, whose brilliant analysis of the Battle of Grahamstown fired my imagination. Walking with her on occasions through the forests of the Fish River valley and the desolate coast of Cove Rock has deepened my appreciation of the history of the Xhosa. The book has also benefited from the help of numerous people including all those who gave up their time, agreed to be interviewed, and trusted me with their opinions and experiences. I am particularly grateful to Kate Rowntree, who helped me find the source of the Kowie River, Chris Mann, whose poems about the river have been inspirational, and Helen Bradford, who gave much advice and spent hours in the Cape Town archives looking for photographs for this book. Thanks also to Candace Feit, Jo and Jaxon Rice and David Stott for the wonderful photographs, and all the other friends who read the whole or parts of the manuscript and commented helpfully, including Eddie Webster, David Fig, Glenn Moss, Georgina Jaffe, Malvern van Wyk Smith, Patricia Milliken, Nicholas Scarr, Michelle Williams, Vishwas Satgar, Dorothy Driver, Karl von Holdt, Tony Dold, Judith Hawarden and Kathie Satchwell. Several friends helped with difficult technical issues, especially Karin Pampallis, Brittany Kesselman and Ingrid Chunwill. I am also very grateful for the comments of two anonymous reviewers, which were extremely helpful, to my editor, Russell Martin, and to Hazel Cuthbertson and Roshan Cader of Wits University Press.

Rivers have the power to connect us to nature, to our past and to our collective selves. They sustain life, inspire poetry and fire our imaginations. As the young sailor in Joseph Conrad's *Heart of Darkness* expressed it, they carry with them 'the dreams of men, the seeds of commonwealth, the germs of empires'.[1] Conrad clearly had in mind the great river highways such as the Amazon, the Congo, the Mississippi, the Mekong, the Thames and the Yangtze. This book tells the story of what is in comparison a 'little' estuarine river, which nevertheless raises large questions.

This river, the Kowie, is not a major waterway and has not been the subject of any scholarly attention. While located in a war-ravaged frontier area, it was never an official frontier and it played a humbler role in South African history than the rivers which the colonial authorities used to mark the changing borders of the Cape Colony: the Bushmans, Fish, Keiskamma and Kei. The area was an open frontier until 1778, when the Fish was declared the official limit of the Cape Colony. Most importantly for this book, the Kowie River runs through the centre of the Zuurveld, the area first bounded by the Fish to the east and the Bushmans to the west.

This was an area of blending and mixing, a meeting point not only of river and sea, of fresh and salt water, but of very different people, identities and traditions that have shaped South African history: Khoikhoi herders, Xhosa pastoralists, Dutch cattle farmers and British settlers. Their interaction often involved intense and violent encounters and still today there are contesting claims and traditions relating to the land, the fertile sour-grass hills and plains of the Zuurveld, now known as Ndlambe Municipal Area, one of the poorest parts of South Africa.

The original inhabitants of the Zuurveld were the Khoikhoi, often contemptuously called 'Hottentots' by the settlers. These indigenous people were the first to experience what has been described as the 'violent, even genocidal process' of colonial expansion in the late eighteenth century as Dutch farmers appropriated their land, their cattle and their power. In 1774 the Dutch government at the Cape ordered that 'the whole race of Bushmen and Hottentots who had not submitted to servitude ... be seized or extirpated'.[2] 'By the end of the century there were no independent living pastoral Khoekhoe in the region.'[3] It was from the Khoi language that the name of the Kowie River derives. The different names given to the river reflect changing constellations of power. According to the *Dictionary of South African English*, Kowie comes from the Khoi word *qohi*, which roughly means 'pipe', an image which could refer to the shape of the river. An early traveller, Ensign Beutler, described how the Khoikhoi smoked their tobacco with a water pipe. According to another authority, the river was called *iCoyi*, from a Khoi word meaning 'buffalo', which used to be numerous in the Kowie valley.[4] In the Eastern Cape, 'it is the rivers that have clung most tenaciously to their Khoi names: Kowie, Kariega, Kei, Keiskamma and Koonap'.[5]

Rivers like the Kowie were important in Khoikhoi identity. According to Ensign Beutler, whose expedition of 1752 passed through the area, the Khoikhoi 'do not know of what people they are: they name themselves only after the rivers by which they live'.[6] He also observed that before they 'cross a big river, they first throw into it a green twig, with wishes to themselves for much luck, a multitude of cattle and long life. Afterwards they wash their whole body and then cross the river.'[7]

Although it is clear from Beutler's journal that there were no Xhosa living west of the Keiskamma at the time of his 1752 expedition, the

Dutch explorer Colonel Robert Gordon found many Xhosa living in the Zuurveld when he visited the area in 1777. By this time, Dutch trekboers, or pastoralists, were already encroaching upon Xhosa and Khoi territory, and within a few years the Zuurveld became marked by struggles over access to land and cattle. The clashes formed the start of what has been called a Hundred Years War between the Xhosa and the colonists, who, after the Cape was taken over by the British, could call on the support of the British army.

The thick bush of the Kowie and other river valleys was the scene of violent clashes during these wars of dispossession. At that time the riverbanks were thick with ancient cycads, wild crane flowers, gigantic yellowwood trees and shady white milkwoods. The dense vegetation, the thickly forested valleys and deep ravines, the towering trees, creepers and vines, all offered hiding places to the Xhosa, for whom this was a familiar landscape. It also made movement difficult for the British soldiers. During one war 'the Gqunukhwebe showed what could be done with the river beds of lower Albany. Using the banks as parapets, they exposed only their heads ... They were able to hide for long periods under water, their nostrils emerging under cover of the reeds at the river's edge. Otherwise they hid in trees, in antbear holes and in caves.'[8] The Kowie was one of the rivers used in this way.

As this history shows, the various groups living in the Zuurveld – Khoikhoi, Xhosa, Dutch and British – interacted not only among themselves but also with the Kowie River in different ways. As with the Khoikhoi, for the Xhosa rivers were geographical markers of identity. Moreover, the Xhosa believed they had sacred qualities. Traditionally Xhosa warriors purified themselves before battle by bathing in rivers. Rivers like the Kowie with their deep pools also provided access to the ancestors, the *Abantu Bomlambo* (People of the River), elusive water divinities who have the power to shape the lives of their descendants. Different pools of the Kowie River were, and are, especially good places for accessing the People of the River. They are believed to live beneath the water with their crops and cattle. Initiates who are called by the ancestors to become diviners go to the People of the River, who sanction their calling. In the millenarian Cattle Killing of 1856–7, according to legend, the People of the River emerged from the water to instruct the Xhosa to purify their contaminated homesteads. Today gifts for the People of the River are often floated out into the centre of river pools in small reed baskets containing items such as sorghum, tobacco, pumpkin seeds and white beads. I have seen offerings to the river people in beautifully woven grass baskets floating in the Blaauwkrantz pool, at the foot of the Blaauwkrantz Gorge, and in the pool that marks the confluence of the Lushington and Kowie rivers. These are places that feel holy and enchanted.

Researching the history of the Kowie has meant revisiting my own ancestors and engaging with their relationship with the river. This engagement is necessary because the ravages of the past continue in the present and, as Aubrey Matshiqi has written, 'the lack of acknowledgement of what was done to black people during the colonial and apartheid eras is a recipe for social, political and economic calamity'.[9]

Acknowledging that past and the inter-generational, racialised privileges it established and perpetuated is one reason why this book is also a personal account of what the river represents to me. As the artist Louise Bourgeois wrote of her childhood, the river weaves 'like a wool thread through everything'.[10] For me, the Kowie River connects a personal and a collective history, the social and the ecological, the sacred and the profane, in both the honouring and the abuse of nature.

This book focuses on three very different moments in the river's story which involved the linked processes of ecological damage and racialised dispossession. The Battle of Grahamstown, which was fought in the vicinity of the Kowie in 1819, changed the course of South African history by consolidating British control of the Zuurveld. In its aftermath, a settlement was established at the mouth of the Kowie River, known as Port Kowie, though it was soon renamed Port Frances by settlers anxious to win favour with the Cape governor, Lord Charles Somerset, whose daughter-in-law was called Frances. Subsequently, it was given yet another name by settlers eager for government support for development of the harbour – Port Alfred, in honour of the British queen's second-eldest son, who toured South Africa in 1860. As the prince chose to go elephant hunting instead of attending the ceremonial renaming of the town, my great-aunt Harriet Cock, then aged 8, deputised for him.

It is the harbour, begun at the river mouth in 1821 and extended and altered through to the 1870s, that forms the second 'moment' of the Kowie River's history explored in this book. The establishment of the harbour helped draw the former Zuurveld region tightly into the trading and commercial networks of the British empire, and contributed in this way to the subjection of the Xhosa within colonial society.

The third moment of my story is the development of an upmarket marina at Port Alfred in 1989. This project has undermined the ecological integrity of the river and at the same time has highlighted and entrenched even further the longstanding divisions in the area between white privilege and black poverty.

Writing the story of the Kowie River has been more than an intellectual engagement. It is both a memoir and a paean to place, a love story disguised as a social and environmental history. When we talk of a 'love of place', Rebecca Solnit points out, we 'usually mean our love for places, but seldom of how the places love us back, of what they give us. They give us continuity, something to return to, and offer a familiarity that allows some portion of our own lives to remain connected and coherent. They give us an expansive scale in which our troubles are set into context, in which the largeness of the world is a balm to loss, trouble and ugliness.'[11]

The Kowie River has given me a great deal. I love the rich prawn smell of the mud banks exposed at low tide, the banks of euphorbia trees, the deep green pools where catfish, giant kob and grunter still live, and the surging tide where the river enters the Indian Ocean. To use the words of the Polish poet Czesław Miłosz, 'we return to the banks of certain rivers',[12] and since infancy there has never been a year when I have not swum in the green-brown waters of the Kowie River, walked its wooded banks or spent hours watching the surge of the tide and the crashing waves as it empties into the sea. In all of these ways – canoeing, swimming, fishing, birdwatching, picnicking or simply sitting on its banks watching the light change – the Kowie River has been a constant thread, a source of renewal of energy and purpose for over seventy years of a tangled life. Going to 'the Kowie' became a kind of pilgrimage, a place to journey to receive the river's spirit and be nourished.

In relation to the lagoon adjoining the east bank of the river, this pearly haze of happy memories is infused with a sense of loss. Like many other local children, I learned to swim in the shallow waters of the lagoon, to drive a car on the lagoon flats and to dance in the adjoining café. This lagoon and an adjoining salt marsh no longer exist. The complex architecture of the salt marsh, a maze of channels kept clear by the sluicing action of the tides, has now been obliterated, replaced by a marina, an exclusive gated community of luxurious houses, many of them holiday homes. In the 1950s, when I grew up, Port Alfred was a very different place, a little fishing village where a horn would blow to signal a catch of fish from the returning boats, fresh produce at the market or the escape of a 'lunatic' from the mental hospital below my parents' house. But the Kowie River and the little town on its banks remain for me a site of density and depth, a connection to ancestral shades and a web of social bonds.

For a long time I have cherished the ambition to traverse the seventy kilometres from the source of the Kowie River to the sea. This ambition to walk and canoe the entire length of the river is inspired by various accounts in river literature. One of the historians of the Thames, Frederick Thacker, maintained that to appreciate 'the ancient and unspoilt countryside' you must 'traverse its roads upon your own feet and pull and steer your craft along its winding reaches with your own arms'.[13] Another inspirational example on a grand scale is Jeremy Seal's attempt to follow the Meander in Turkey for five hundred kilometres from its headwaters at Dinar to the Aegean with his collapsible canoe.[14] Another intrepid adventurer was Phil Harwood, who braved crocodiles, giant snakes and angry locals to become the first person to canoe the Congo River from its source in a tiny spring at the base of a banyan tree in the highlands of Zambia until it finally enters the ocean five thousand kilometres away.[15]

I have drawn on a rich river literature, from T.S. Eliot's Thames in *The Waste Land*, (so different from the Thames of Kenneth Grahame's *Wind in the Willows*), Paul Horgan's Rio Grande, James Joyce's Liffey, Alan Moorhead's and Robert Trigger's Nile, Joseph Conrad's and Tim Butcher's Congo, Mark Twain's Mississippi, Charles Dodgson's Isis and Joan McGregor's Zambezi, to mention a few works with which I am familiar. Most scholarly is Simon Winchester's journey down the Yangtze in *The River at the Centre of the World*. I was moved by the redoubtable Isabella Bird's account of her voyage through the Yangtze Gorge and fascinated by Peter Ackroyd's description of the 250-mile length of the Thames, though the short distance I've managed walking along a well-signposted Thames path with cows and green fields could not have been more different from my home experience. I was also inspired by Olivia Laing's account of her walk along Virginia Woolf's river, the Ouse, in which she drowned herself. This book is a wonderful account of how history resides in a landscape. I could identify with Laing's feelings for the Ouse, the 'river I've returned to over and again, in sickness and in health, in grief, in desolation and in joy'.[16]

Following the course of the Kowie through what used to be the Zuurveld and trying to access the 'deep history' of the area is also troubling because of my knowledge of what has occurred there, of earlier calamities. As Robert Macfarlane has written of walking through areas of Scotland subjected to the Highland Clearances: 'The pasts of these places complicate and darken their present wildness ... To be in such landscapes is to be caught in a double-bind: how is it possible to love them in the present, but also to acknowledge their troubled histories?'[17] At the same time as the Clearances were taking place, the indigenous

Xhosa people of the Zuurveld were being driven from their homes and subjected to the same violent process of dispossession as the Scottish crofters. So researching this book has forced me to acknowledge the 'double-bind'.

Yet, if one can banish these ghosts of the past, the Kowie River catchment (the area of land drained by the river) is a colourful place. In summer the landscape is bright with the scarlet flowers of the coral tree and the pink blooms of Cape chestnut trees. In winter whole hillsides are ablaze with thickets of orange aloes, as well as the crane flower. Orange is the iconic Zuurveld colour, as it is also the colour of the traditional Xhosa dress dyed by using local clay.

Over the years I have explored much of the Kowie by foot or canoe. This was generally marvellous fun, though bad timing sometimes meant canoeing against the wind and tides, and traipsing through dense thickets of bush. The banks of the Kowie are lush in places with giant yellowwood trees and cycads, but elsewhere it is flanked by scrub and thornbush. It is not a showy, dramatic landscape. On one occasion I nearly trod on a cobra but its warning hiss saved me. Another time, in a stupid moment of exhaustion I lay down on my back under a milk-wood on the grassy riverbank and was instantly covered by an invasion of tiny 'pepper ticks'. Once I set out with two intrepid friends to walk a stretch of the river north of Bathurst from Penny's Hoek to Waters Meeting. This involved wading across the river (with the fast-flowing water waist-high) and fighting through reeds which stretched over our heads. We stopped frequently to keep our strength up with chocolate biscuits and tea made on a tiny gas stove. Though we carried Google Earth maps of the area, we argued endlessly about our exact location and eventually turned back. Given that our ages varied from 65 to 71 and between us all we were taking medication for high blood pressure, cancer, high cholesterol levels or diabetes, the attempt was a sort of geriatric heroics.

To find the source of the Kowie, I needed the help of a geographer. We eventually located it in a patch of dense indigenous forest in a ravine in the hills surrounding Grahamstown, called Featherstone Kloof. This muddy, leaf-choked spot is not a dramatic birthplace. There was none of the sense of mystery and power sometimes reported of springs and river sources in classical mythology. As Olivia Laing wrote of the Ouse, 'there was no spring. The water didn't bubble from the ground ... "*the source*" sounded a grand name for this clammy runnel.'[18] But I understood Robert Twigger's 'sense of contentment' as he glimpsed 'the small puddle in the middle of the jungle in Rwanda', the spot earlier explorers had decided was the 'real, true source of the Nile'.[19] At the time we made our discovery near Grahamstown, it was an extraordinary thought that the thin, brown trickle of water could transform itself into the tumultuous river which at its ocean mouth has caused fishermen to drown and boats to overturn.

So why should we be concerned about this little river? There is nothing grand or magnificent about the Kowie, though its beauty has been recorded by artists such as Thomas Bowler, Frederick I'Ons and Marianne North. David Harvey answers the question: 'In the broad scheme of things, the disappearance of a wetland here, a local species there and a particular habitat somewhere else may seem trivial as well as inevitable given the imperatives of human population growth, let alone the continuity of endless capital accumulation at a compound rate. But it is precisely the aggregation of such small-scale changes that can produce macro-ecological problems such as global deforestation, loss of habitat and biodiversity, desertification and oceanic pollution.'[20] This book shows how the Kowie River is implicated in such social, political, economic and 'macro-ecological problems'.

What did the Kowie River area look like in the past? Who were the original inhabitants and how did they live? Who was the Khoikhoi leader Captain Ruyter? Who were Makhanda and Ndlambe and what happened to them? When did the early European travellers – men like Le Vailliant with his plumed hat and his pet baboon and William Burchell with his fifty reference books, his flute and Khoi servants – visit this area and what did they think of it? What role did the 1820 settlers play in the region and, in particular, one of their number who was my great-great-grandfather William Cock? How important was the Kowie River to the development of the Eastern Cape? In recent times, was the breaching of the riverbanks to establish a marina a pioneering model of sustainable growth providing employment for a desperately poor community and making increasing revenue from rates available for development? Or was it a form of 'ecocide', which involved the destruction of a significant wetland and damaged the river irreparably? Both the harbour and the marina were established in the name of 'development', but did the benefits extend beyond a wealthy elite? These are some of the questions this book addresses.

* * *

Sitting quietly at places like the confluence of the Kowie and Lushington rivers, or canoeing or walking through the riverine forest, involves encounters with wild nature. One can hear the lap of the tide, and perhaps the bark of a bushbuck or the coughing sound of a baboon. Birdsong is constant and might include the sweet notes of the Black-headed Oriole, or the harsh alarm call of the Knysna Loerie, flying away with its scarlet underwings flashing, or even the soft hooting of the shy Narina Trogon. There are kingfishers and rare waterbirds like the African Finfoot and the Green-backed Heron. These birds are our access to nature, to the wild and the pristine. I have watched Cape Clawless Otters at play in a gold dawn light. These are very intimate and privileged experiences of wild nature. They give us the space (both psychic and geographical) to think about our place in the world and our relations with the wild creatures with whom we share it. They can remind us of our place in nature, of our ecological interdependence, even of our dependence on the trees which release the oxygen that allow us to live. They can provide us with a sense of joy, 'an intense happiness'.[21] Olive Schreiner wrote of 'that strange impersonal peace that comes into our hearts when we contemplate nature'.[22] It can also involve focusing and simplifying our lives. Henry David Thoreau believed: 'in Wildness is the preservation of the World'.[23] For him, walking ('sauntering' he called it) was the best way of connecting with nature. In a spirit of pilgrimage, I visited Walden Pond in Massachusetts where Thoreau lived, but today, filled with crowds and cars, Walden is a very different place.

Just as Walden Pond represented the world for Thoreau, the Kowie River embodies much of what I care about. So writing this book has involved three kinds of journeys: firstly, intellectual in the research process, which has involved many conversations and interviews with very different people as well as solitary hours in archives and reading rooms trying to trace the history of the area and understand its earliest inhabitants – the Khoikhoi, Dutch, Xhosa and British. Secondly, it has involved many physical journeys down the river, from its rising near Grahamstown to its Indian Ocean mouth, often retracing well-loved bays and places. Both these journeys of exploration have been fun. But the book has also involved an emotional journey, which has raised some unsettling questions about my own ancestry.

One of the British 1820 settlers was my great-great-grandfather. In my family he was always referred to as the Honourable William Cock, the name spoken in deferential tones, as if the title signalled more than membership of a discredited colonial institution, the Legislative Council, whose members were appointed by the governor of the Cape Colony. In these family conversations he was invariably described as an entrepreneur, and his efforts to turn the Kowie River into a productive harbour were always framed as a heroic confrontation with the forces of nature. It was therefore deeply shocking for me to read of him in recent historians' accounts as a member of a settler elite who promoted the violent dispossession of the land and livelihoods of the indigenous population. Was William Cock a warmonger and profiteer, 'the army butcher' as the historian Timothy Keegan describes him? Was he one of the 'strangers to honour', as Noël Mostert terms the 1820 settler elite, or a brave pioneer and entrepreneur? The developer of the Port Alfred marina told me, 'William Cock is the father of the marina. We could not

have done it without him.' This book will show that there are similar-
ities in the two main assaults on the integrity of the Kowie River: the
nineteenth-century harbour and the modern marina. Both are linked
to a process of racialised dispossession originating in the violence of
settler colonialism.

Obviously I found it painful to consider my revered great-great-
grandfather as part of an imperialist settler elite driven by narrow
commercial interests at best, a warmonger and profiteer at worst.
But this was not the only unsettling discovery about my own family
during the course of researching this book. I used to love working
in the heavy, comfortable silence of museums and reading rooms.
But the sense of peaceful engagement with the past was shattered in
a particularly uncomfortable discovery one day. Going through old
papers in the reading room of the Albany Museum in Grahamstown,
I came across a letter which contained a reference to my mother, for
whose intellect and integrity I had great respect. The writer stated,
'I have come to the conclusion that Mrs Pauline Cock is a very unre-
liable source of settler history. What she doesn't know she simply
invents.' Part of what she 'invented' was a consoling narrative held
by many descendants of the 1820 settlers who still live in the Kowie
area, one that tends to idolise the courage and enterprise of the settlers
and praise the extension of the benefits of British civilisation to the
benighted Xhosa.

Rivers can connect us not only to nature, from which many urban
people are alienated, but also to questions of justice. Understanding
that we are all part of nature in the food we eat, the water we drink and
the air we breathe means recognising both our ecological and social
interdependence and our shared vulnerability. Furthermore, rivers
can connect us to our past and show how it is inscribed in the present.
Researching the Kowie River has involved revisiting my own ancestors
and confronting the inter-generational privilege which forms part of
their legacy. This has meant confronting many prejudices, myths and
distortions, which this book describes.

My story of the Kowie River acknowledges how the ravages of the past continue to flow through the present. It is a story that incorporates both social and environmental injustice: the silting and pollution of a river and the violent conquest of the indigenous Xhosa whose descendants continue to live in poverty and material deprivation.

But around the world people are increasingly reconnecting with nature and justice through rivers. Unlike other bodies of water, such as dams, oceans and lakes, rivers have a destination and we can learn from the strength and certainty with which they travel. I believe this learning is valuable because acknowledging the past, and the inter-generational, racialised privileges, damages and denials it established and perpetuates, is necessary for any shared future.

2 | The Kowie River

The Kowie is an ancient river; it flows through land where dinosaurs once roamed and where cycads still grow. At one time this land was covered by the sea with marine deposits fifty million years old. It is a wild, tidal river, dynamic, forever changing and diverse. This diversity lies not only in the different types of country through which it flows, but also in the changing seasons, the differences between wet and dry years, between high and low tides, and the rich variety of the forms of life it sustains. The Kowie River has not received scholarly attention from historians, nor has its beauty been acknowledged by poets or writers, except for one noteworthy exception. In his poem 'The Rivers' (1982), Chris Mann celebrates this diversity:

> The rivers of the Eastern Cape are full of hidden life:
>> quiet cob, greenyblackcrab,
>> turtle and tadpole flimmer and flee;
> The rivers of the Eastern Cape are walked by recent ghosts:
>> waterbuck, lithebuck leopard doe;
> The rivers of the Eastern Cape run with holy waters:
>> ochred priest and prophet refract
>> the shimmershades in pools.[1]

The term 'holy waters' refers to the enduring and sacred importance of the Kowie River to many Xhosa people today.

* * *

One of my most magical river moments was at dawn one morning in 2005 as I was crouching in the lush vegetation lining the beautiful deep green pool that marks the confluence of the Kowie and Lushington rivers. A friend and I were waiting to see the otters whose holt I had discovered in this particular pool. After sitting motionless for a long time, we saw the whiskered head of an otter break the surface and then turn, swimming on her back with a crab in her front paws, followed by three otter cubs. My friend and I didn't move or speak, but after a while the golden silence was broken by the sound of rhythmic chanting and the beat of a drum. Five figures, all clothed in white, their faces painted with white clay and their heads covered in white cloth turbans, suddenly appeared. They were led by a diviner in a white robe and red turban carrying a flywhisk in one hand and a spear in the other. We watched in fascination as they removed their shoes and chanted to the rhythm of a cowhide drum, calling in sonorous tones on 'the People of the River', the source of the created world. The experience felt like the 'shining adventure' which the conservationist Aldo Leopold described while canoeing through the 'milk and honey wilderness' of the Colorado River delta in the 1920s.

I later learned that this was a pool where certain water divinities reside. We had been privileged to witness one of the rituals (*intlwayalelo*) associated with the induction of a traditional diviner-healer. According to Xhosa cosmology, the sighting of otters makes for an especially auspicious occasion because otters are messengers (*izithunywa*) from the ancestors. Seeing otters swimming, fish jumping, birds calling, ducks quacking or leguaans splashing in the water or near a riverbank is regarded as a positive sign in the *intlwayalelo* ritual. I learned this, and much else, years later from the research by the social anthropologist Penny Bernard, who had visited this particular place for her study of water divinities.

In Xhosa cosmology the Kowie, along with all rivers, is regarded as spiritually significant. It has several sacred pool sites, the deep pools favoured by water divinities or river spirits. These are the 'People of the River' (*Abantu Bomlambo* in isiXhosa). They are sometimes described as mermaids (half fish, half human beings) and are associated with pools situated deep in forests. All the Kowie River pools I have explored are very deep, remote and difficult to access, surrounded by dense vegetation and often by precipitous cliffs, as in the case of the Lushington pool, the site of my 'shining adventure'. Pools where the water divinities are thought to reside are classified as sacred because they are regarded as 'sites that have an intensified presence of the ancestors and the divine forces'.[2]

The People of the River play a pivotal role in the calling, initiation and final induction of Xhosa diviner-healers (*amagqirha*). Called to their work by the ancestors, they possess supernatural powers which enable them to determine the causes of misfortune or illness and the required form of propitiation. Following a calling from the ancestors to the river, a trainee undergoes a lengthy period of apprenticeship to an established diviner.

This training involves three traditional rituals. Firstly, there is the *intlwayalelo*, a term derived from the verb meaning 'to sow seeds'. These rites involve various offerings: white clay, medicinal roots, white beads, pumpkin seeds, grains of sorghum and maize, tobacco and the body dirt (*intsila*) of the candidate (*umkwetha*) undergoing induction. To connect the novice diviner-healer and his living kin to their ancestors, the offerings are best made at dawn at a river pool. Bernard reports seeing small baskets or tin lids containing a mixture of seeds floating near reedbeds at a number of recognised sacred pool sites in the area. I have seen them frequently but have only learned recently of these rituals' multifaceted significance; for example, the drumming my friend and I heard is meant to keep the ancestors awake.

The poet Chris Mann compares the diviners to the oracles of ancient Greece and Rome, and writes, 'prayers, songs and imprecations follow, all the more affecting since they are made by the people of a culture which, despite the advent of democracy in South Africa, is still struggling with the effects of conquest, dispossession, poverty and migrant labour'.[3] Mann goes on to note that 'it is a deeply humanizing experience in this context to reread Odysseus' account of his visit to the underworld in the *Iliad*'. I was reminded of Elizabeth Bishop's poem 'The Riverman' (1965), an intense account of an Amazonian villager being called below the water by a powerful river spirit:

> I got up in the night
> for the Dolphin spoke to me …
> Godfathers and cousins,
> your canoes are over my head;
> I hear your voices talking.
> You can peer down and down
> or dredge the river bottom
> but never, never catch me …
> The Dolphin singled me out …[4]

In southern Africa as a whole there are many references to diviner-healers who claim to have been taken underwater to receive skills, wisdom and medicine in order to return and heal the living. Physical submersion signifies a higher level of skill for the diviner, but 'most diviners and their initiates merely dreamed about being submerged in the river'.[5]

In the early 1940s a man with the name of Tyota was called to the Kowie River by his ancestors. In his case the message was brought by two Nile Monitors (*Varanus niloticus*, or *uxam* in isiXhosa), also known as leguaans, who followed him like pet dogs when he was walking in the veld, a sign of his impending calling to the river. 'The Nile Monitor is reputedly the herdsman of the river people, driving their cattle out of the river under the cover of mist at dawn to graze in the grasslands and herding them back under the river at sunset.'[6] Tyota spoke of a bright light emanating from the Kowie River that put him into a trance and of meeting an old woman 'half human and half fish'.

Being called by a leguaan is not uncommon. Leguaans are one of the river creatures, along with crabs and otters, who are messengers from the ancestors. Near the Lushington pool I have often seen them, the largest of the African lizards, growing up to 200 cm in length. They have an intimidating prehistoric appearance, with a stout body, strong claws and a long tail.

The anthropological literature seems confusing on the relationship between the water divinities and the ancestors. According to Tony Dold (based on research in the Eastern Cape), these water divinities are regarded as ancestors, whereas according to Penny Bernard they are intermediaries and both they and the ancestors live in the sacred pools and work in close association. The ancestors and the river people cooperate; they work together, especially in the calling of diviner-healers.

According to one Xhosa source from the Kowie area, the People of the River are highly temperamental and easily angered. 'Abantu Bomlambo are our ancestors, we do not know their names but we know them. They live in the river and in the sea. They visit us in the ubuhlanti [animal pen] at night and take care of us. If we disturb them in the river they become angry with us. We need to be on good terms. Sometimes children playing near the river throw stones in the river and the people of the river are disturbed and become angry.'[7]

There are many reports that these traditional diviners and healers have survived the advent of modernity and can be found not only in every rural settlement but in every urban township. The pool sites they frequent have an ecological as well as a spiritual significance for many indigenous people. The spirit world is regarded as the ultimate source of life-sustaining resources. But 'sacred pool sites of key significance for healers are being systematically threatened by development projects, mining and modern agricultural practices. The privatisation of land has led to many of the sacred pools being inaccessible to healers.'[8] Furthermore, channelling water from rivers can upset the water shades. Traditional taboos exist regarding natural resources, such as not collecting firewood near rivers, to avoid disturbing the water divinities. The Lushington pool has been fenced by the local farmer and the water is piped to irrigate his fields. The throb of the irrigation pump is an affront to the deep silence of the place. In these ways the meanings embedded in indigenous culture are disregarded.

The river rituals of the Xhosa are still widely practised. In fact, one of the strongest lines of continuity in this river story is the respect the river still inspires among many in the Xhosa population. Obviously it would be wrong to essentialise or generalise about such a large category of people, but for many of the Xhosa still living near the Kowie the area is more than an important source of food, fuel, medicine and building material. Behind such utilitarian use lies a deep traditional appreciation of nature. As Dold and Cocks write in their book, *Voices from the Forest*, which celebrates the link between people and nature or, as they frame it, between cultural and biological diversity (sometimes called 'biocultural diversity'), both rural and urban South Africans still find great cultural and spiritual value in nature. 'The *isiXhosa* language portrays nature (*indalo*) in idioms, proverbs, traditional riddles, songs and the names and descriptions of times of the day, months of the year and seasons of the year. The poetry of these is self-evident.'[9] This is wonderfully clear in Xhosa birdlore, where the names and idioms reflect closely observed and deep ornithological knowledge and appreciation. An example is the Hamerkop (*uqhimngqofe*), which symbolises vanity from its habit of remaining for hours at the water's edge, where it is supposed to be admiring its reflection, or the Narina Trogon, whose stationary habits indicate laziness.[10]

Many indigenous societies have such a non-dualistic view of nature and culture, with traditions of resource use that include spiritual attachment and knowledge that involves a conservation ethic. Among the Xhosa the link between the 'natural' and the 'cultural' is maintained by respect for the ancestors, and several informants believed that environmental damage is disrespectful to the ancestors. Many traditional cultural practices of the Xhosa make regular and highly controlled use of wild plants and animals. Research in one area reports that activities that brought them into 'regular contact' with nature, such as collecting firewood, hunting and being secluded in initiation schools, were important opportunities for spending time with nature.[11] The forest was especially valued 'as a place that bestows spiritual health and well-being (*impila*)'. One informant said, 'sometimes I walk with my dog or hunt in the forest, or I just sit in a quiet place to forget my worries.'[12]

This appreciation contrasts with much of local people's experience of environmental conservation authorities and practices intent on the exclusion of people and on the strict, legalistic control of natural resources. The outcome of this 'fences and fines' approach has been that – especially under apartheid and colonial rule – environmentalism was somewhat questioned, as it was concerned only with the protection of threatened plants, animals and wilderness areas, to the neglect of human needs. Furthermore, the dispossession of rural people to create protected areas illustrates the brutality involved. As Cocks writes, 'approaches to conserving biodiversity that are based on cultural and religious values are often more sustainable than those based only on legislation or regulation'.[13]

Two Rockys

The water divinities are not the only magical creatures associated with the Kowie River. Unlike other parts of southern Africa, the river does not sustain owls that fish, but there are kingfishers, which are insectivorous, and air-breathing fish.

One of the first air-breathing fish to be described scientifically, *Sandelia bainsii*, the Eastern Cape Rocky, was from the Kowie River. These fish have accessory breathing organs so that they can breathe atmospheric air as we do, for where they lie there is often not enough oxygen in the water to use only their gills. According to Jim Cambray, the former Albany Museum director, in the last twenty years the numbers of this species have dwindled dramatically, and it is 'almost extinct'.[14] It is a true Eastern Cape resident. The genus was named after King Sandile (1820–78), who was the son of Ngqika, king of the Rharhabe section of the Xhosa nation in the Eastern Cape. The species name also honours the geologist Andrew Geddes Bain (1797–1864), who built many roads in the Eastern Cape and found some important fossils. The fish is endemic to several rivers in the Eastern Cape but was first described from the Kowie River. It likes quiet rocky habitats where it wedges itself between rocks or submerged logs and waits for prey items like crabs or small fishes to float or swim past. The fish features in a poster by Maggie Newman sponsored by the Albany Museum showing forty animal species, local vegetation and underwater life, so as to depict the interrelationships between animals and plants in the terrestrial and aquatic ecosystems of the Kowie catchment area. The poster setting is a pool in the Blaauwkrantz Nature Reserve, an area set aside for the conservation of the Eastern Cape Rocky. Unfortunately, the aquatic weed *Azolla* now completely covers the pool's surface, making it difficult for people to place gifts for the ancestors in the water. The pool is commonly known as *kwatiki*, after the small 'tickey' coin. According to Tony Dold, there was once a toll over the Blaauwkrantz bridge which charged a tickey to cross.

A rare white line

Before human intervention, the lower Kowie estuary consisted of a number of channels and sandbanks that migrated across the floodplain. In such estuaries the interaction between sea and river creates unique and dynamic ecosystems. Estuaries are a type of wetland, the planet's most productive ecosystems. Wetlands and other estuary-associated habitats perform important services. Water draining the catchment area carries sediments and pollutants, which are filtered out or trapped by marginal vegetation and salt marshes. Coastal plants (like salt marshes) represent a significant contribution to carbon sequestration, popularly known as blue carbon.[15]

Estuaries 'support critical habitats such as salt marshes, intertidal mud and sandbanks, and eel grass beds which are used by many species

1. The source of the Kowie River is 70 km inland among the densely forested ravines in the hills surrounding Grahamstown. There is a capillary of streams and water points including the famous spring (*umthombo*) that flows constantly with sweet water (Photograph: Kate Rowntree).

2. The sacred pool at the confluence of the Kowie and Lushington rivers where tributes such as white beads or pumpkin seeds are sometimes floated in small reed baskets for the *Abantu Bomlambo* (People of the River) (Photograph: Candace Feit).

3. Initiates at the Lushington pool. The *Abantu Bomlambo* play a pivotal role in the calling, initiation and induction of Xhosa diviner-healers (*amagqirha*) (Photograph: Helen Bradford).

4. The Blaauwkrantz pool, at the foot of the Blaauwkrantz Gorge, is another spiritual place to connect with the water divinities, the *Abantu Bomlambo*, and access the ancestors. Unfortunately the pool's surface is now covered by the aquatic weed *Azolla* (Photograph: Candace Feit).

5. Portrait believed to be of the Xhosa warrior, prophet and philosopher Makhanda/Makana/Nxele, who led his troops against the British army in the Battle of Grahamstown in 1819 (Painting by Frederick Timpson I'Ons, 1835. Albany Museum/Africa Media Online).

6. The Kowie River follows a 'horseshoe bend' between Port Alfred and Bathurst in the Waters Meeting Nature Reserve (so called because that is where the salt water from the Kowie River mouth meets the upstream fresh water) (Photograph: AAI).

7. Before human intervention, the estuary of the Kowie River consisted of a number of channels and sandbanks which were exposed by the retreating tide (Artist unknown, 1822. Cory Library/Africa Media Online).

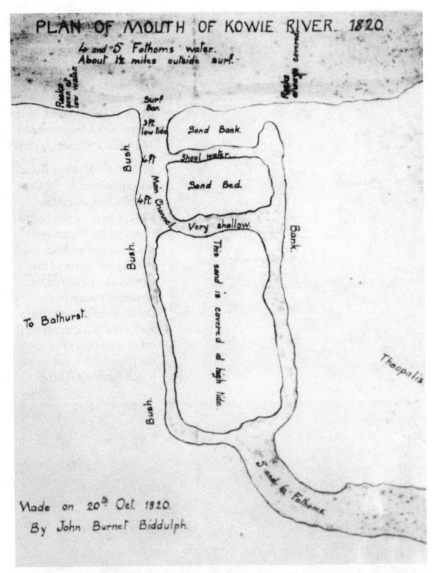

PLAN OF MOUTH OF KOWIE RIVER. 1820

4 and 5 Fathoms water.
About 1½ miles outside surf.

Rocks seen at low water.

Rocks always covered.

Surf Bar.

3 Ft. low tide

Bush.

4 Ft.

Main Channel

4 Ft.

Sand Bank.

Shoal water.

Sand Bed.

Very shallow.

Bank.

Bush.

This sand is covered at high tide.

To Bathurst.

Bush.

Theopalis.

5 and 6 Fathoms.

Made on 20th Oct. 1820.
By John Burnet Biddulph.

8. In 1820 British officer Lieutenant John Biddulph sketched the Kowie River mouth while investigating the possibility of establishing a port there as part of the British colonial agenda. The mouth was partially closed by two sandbars, which meant extreme variations in the level of the water as the tides changed. He established that at the river mouth tides rose sufficiently to admit vessels of up to about 120 tons (Cory Library/Rhodes University).

LEFT: 9. William Cock (1793–1876), the author's great-great-grandfather seen here in 1864, was principally responsible for the development of the harbour at the mouth of the Kowie River, beginning in 1838 (Cock Family Archive).

BELOW: 10. William Cock was appointed to the Cape Legislative Council in 1847, where he worked to promote the expansion of the colony, which involved the dispossession of the Xhosa, and to secure the governor's support for the harbour project. He is seen here (back right) with other members of the Council in 1864 (Cock Family Archive).

11. Under Cock's direction a new mouth was cut for the river through the sand hills of the west bank. The river was canalised and the channel straightened and diverted to the western side of the estuary, producing a navigable stretch of about three-quarters of a mile inland (Date of photograph unknown. Western Cape Archives, AG 1443).

12. Sedimentation was a problem, so to keep the river mouth deep enough, two piers were built in the 1850s extending into the sea. The estuary was regularly dredged to allow the velocity of the tide to flush the mouth and keep the harbour free of sand (Date of photograph unknown. Cory Library/Africa Media Online).

LEFT: 13. Throughout the 1840s the harbour was used by sailing ships, usually small schooners and cutters. Their cargoes were partially offloaded into small boats before they attempted to enter the river. Locally built lighters were used to unload larger vessels anchored out at sea (Date of photograph unknown. Cory Library/Africa Media Online).

ABOVE: 14. The Albany Steam Navigation Company, owned by William Cock, operated the *Sir John St Aubyn*, an iron steamship for cargo and passengers that made its first journey from Cape Town to Port Frances (later Port Alfred) in record time (3½ days) in July 1842 (Painting by Edith Cock, 1840s. Cock Family Archive).

LEFT: 15. Steamship moored in the Kowie River. The harbour development increased trade between the port, Cape Town, England and Mauritius. Ships took cargoes of sheep, butter, beans, grain, hide and tallow to Mauritius and brought back sugar. The harbour was busiest in the 1870s with 101 ships entering in 1876 (Date of photograph unknown. Western Cape Archives, AG 4651).

16. View of the Kowie River by Thomas Bowler, from the flagpole in front of William Cock's house, according to a family member. The view shows the dredger at work in the river (Hand-coloured engraving from original artwork by Thomas Bowler, 1864. Cory Library/Africa Media Online).

17. An artist (probably Thomas Bowler) sits on the East Bank and sketches boats in the harbour. William Cock's residence, Richmond House, is visible on the top of the hill in the distance (Artist and date unknown. Western Cape Archives, L 1545).

LEFT: 18. Letitia Harriet Cock (1852–1951) as a young woman. She was William Cock's eldest granddaughter and the author's great-aunt. She recalled being given the honour, at the age of 8, of christening the town of Port Alfred when its name was changed from Port Frances in 1860 (Date of photograph unknown. Cock Family Archive).

BELOW LEFT: 19. Letitia Harriet Cock in later life. Her reminiscences of frontier life and memories of her grandfather William Cock were a valuable source of oral testimony for the author (Date of photograph unknown. Cock Family Archive).

BELOW: 20. Letitia Harriet Cock with the author. Despite the 90-year age gap, Harriet and the author had an extraordinarily close relationship (1940s) (Cock Family Archive).

21. Early photograph looking across the Kowie River to the East Bank and the Indian Ocean beyond. The area is now covered by the Royal Alfred Marina (Date of photograph unknown. Cory Library/Africa Media Online).

22. The mouth of the Kowie River and the East Bank (left) as they looked in the 1960s before the wetland was destroyed by the marina development in 1989 (Postcard by Protea Colour Prints (Pty) Ltd).

23. The Kowie River mouth showing the canalisation of the river between two piers stretching out into the ocean (Photograph: David Stott).

24. The dunes on the East Bank. To the left of the picture is where silt from the dredging of the marina canals and the estuary is dumped. This affects the natural wave action and migration of the sand dunes (Photograph: David Larsen/Africa Media Online).

25. River view looking upstream, with both banks covered by indigenous vegetation (Date of photograph unknown, possibly early 20th century. Western Cape Archives, E2773).

26. The same view as figure 25 above, in 2017, showing the upmarket housing development, Riverview Waterfront Estate, which destroyed the natural vegetation and blocked public access along the river bank (Photograph: David Stott).

27. Aerial photograph of the town of Port Alfred in the 1960s before the marina development (Postcard by Art Publishers (Pty) Ltd, Umbilo, Durban. Photograph: B. K. Bjornsen).

28. There are currently plans for the construction of another 'high density waterfront marina', Centenary Park, at the bend of the river, on the far right. This will damage the river irreparably (Photograph: David Stott).

29. Overview of the Royal Alfred Marina developed at the mouth of the Kowie River in 1989 by a private developer (Photograph: David Stott).

30. Looking across towards the East Bank. The marina destroyed a wetland, privatised a public asset, and causes ongoing silting in the Kowie River (Photograph: Joanna Rice).

31. The marina consists of 355 upmarket houses each with its own waterfront. They are mostly holiday homes for wealthy upcountry visitors (Photograph: David Stott).

32. Nemato township, Port Alfred. An 8 km walk to the town centre, this is home to thousands of Africans living with high rates of poverty, unemployment, hunger, and uneven and irregular provision of municipal services (Photograph: David Larsen/Africa Media Online).

for foraging and as nursery areas'.[16] Not only fish, but also many species of mammal, bird, fish, crustaceans, insects and other wildlife forms depend on estuaries to survive, eat, reproduce, migrate and live permanently. They are especially important nursery areas for many fish species, such as White Steenbras, Dusky Kob and Spotted Grunter. According to Professor Alan Whitfield, a total of 155 fish species are dependent on South African estuaries: 42 species breed in estuaries, 61 species use estuaries as nurseries, and 103 species are partially or completely dependent on estuaries.

There are only some 250 functioning estuaries in South Africa, and the Kowie estuary is classified as a medium-to-large, permanently open estuary. Nevertheless, the Kowie, as with estuaries in general, has 'been subject to increasing pressure, especially as a result of reductions in river water inflow and increasing development along river banks'.[17]

Human impact since the 1830s has involved the extensive canalisation of the lower reaches of the river: the main channel was straightened and confined within stone walls, and the mouth moved westwards. Today the mouth is an estuary, a narrow, 21 km long stretch of tidal river. The river itself is significantly larger, some 70 km in length. The lower part of the Kowie estuary now consists of an artificial channel, approximately 80 m wide, with loose stone-packed berms.

Two piers have been built at the river mouth, with the west pier much longer than the east. At times at the mouth the river loses itself in the vast space of the ocean, but at high tide with a west wind blowing there is a dramatic meeting. A large sandbar dominates the mouth region, which varies seasonally depending on prevailing winds and swell direction. Locals report that a legendary local fisherman, Ronnie Samuel – who reputedly saved forty people from drowning over the years – once walked across the bar at a spring low tide. Crossing it was, and still is, dangerous and a number of fishermen have experienced 'crossing the bar' as death, rather than metaphor, when their boats overturned.

At times a flooding tide creates a white line of foam in the middle of the river near the mouth. This is often marked by terns diving to feed off the plankton caught up in the circulation. According to the marine biologist Dr Nadine Strydom, 'the white line is caused by a convergence zone created by the meeting of water of different densities in a confined channel. The confined channel is the result of the artificial walling by William Cock when the two piers were constructed. In two other Eastern Cape rivers, the Sundays and the Gamtoos, this occurs naturally whereas in the Kowie it is the result of this artificial walling.'[18]

The Kowie catchment area

Rivers derive much of their character from the catchments through which they flow. The Kowie catchment is the area of land between 576 and 769 km² drained by the river, and the major part of it is made up of privately owned farms. The main agricultural activities of the region involve the production of pineapples, chicory, citrus, fodder crops, beef cattle and goats. The Kowie River is perennial, rising in a patch of dense indigenous forest on the sloping hills surrounding Grahamstown, and flowing steadily through the centre of what used to be called the Zuurveld towards the sea. The 70 km length the river travels from source to sea occurs along a gently sloping coastal plain, a diverse landscape of undulating hills, dense indigenous forest and cultivated farmland. The landscape is best appreciated from the toposcope situated at one of the highest points in Featherstone Kloof outside Grahamstown. From here one has a view of the landscape framed by the Indian Ocean in the south with Port Alfred 43 km away as the crow flies, and the mountains of the Winterberg and the Amatolas in the north. The catchment area contains many small streams which feed into the river and its main tributary, the Blaauwkrantz.

The helpful geographer who directed me to the river's source was somewhat dismissive of my obsession with finding the starting point of the Kowie River. 'It can be a bit difficult to say exactly where the source is, because the source is actually the hill slopes, then the water seeps out somewhere into the channel.' She stressed that one 'should think in terms of the watershed rather than a single source'.[19] These hills contain a capillary of streams and water points including the famous spring (*umthombo* in isiXhosa) which gushes from the hillside next to the main road from Grahamstown to Port Alfred. It flows constantly with wonderfully sweet water. Along with the streams that flow off the north slopes of Signal Hill, it supplied the British soldiers stationed at Fort England with water from as early as 1816. What is now Grahamstown was chosen as the site for a military base because of these hillside streams which drained the north-facing flanks of the Rietberge (later known as Mountain Drive). The earliest water sources of the garrison town were the courses that run into the town from the hills to the south. Small dams diverted the water into furrows. Those that now empty into Grey Dam poured into a wooden trough crossing the Waterkloof 2 (Douglas Dam) stream. From the Drostdy Arch, stone canals led the water down High Street, and each household drew its share from the canals according to a timetable. The storage tank next to the Drostdy Arch, installed in 1818 and restored in 1979, permitted an extension to the system.[20]

The stream, known as the Kowie Ditch, which flows through Grahamstown, is cemented, canalised and heavily polluted in places as it dribbles through the little town. This is the Blaauwkrantz, which rises near the old golf course, close to the road to the army base, and flows past Fort England. The Blaauwkrantz is the largest of the Kowie River's tributaries. Others are the Lushington (also known as the Torrens) and the Mansfield and Bathurst streams.

There are also a number of smaller, unnamed streams entering the river along its course. There are several deep pools, such as Cambray's pool at the foot of the Blaauwkrantz Pass, and that marking the confluence of the Lushington and Kowie rivers at the place I call 'the green cathedral'. In places the Lushington is densely lined with palm trees (*Phoenix reclinata*), close relatives of the North African date palm. These plants are the southernmost naturally occurring palms in the world.

Where the Kowie River passes through the Tyson pineapple farm half-way to Grahamstown, it is locally known by Xhosa people as 'the deep place'.

The Kowie is no longer a working river, though a century ago it was a harbour for ocean-going boats and served to drive the mills on its banks grinding wheat into flour and, in the case of Bradshaw's Mill, built in 1823 on the small tributary of the Bathurst stream, weaving wool into rough cloth. Today the Kowie supplies local farmers with water for irrigation and the domestic water needs of the little town of Port Alfred from the Sarel Hayward Dam. For a long time, the river was crossed by ferry until a pontoon was erected in 1876 and the present bridge in 2007.

The river is tidal as far as Ebb and Flow, which is the place where salt and fresh waters meet 21 km upstream from the mouth. The river is navigable by small boats almost up to this point. Paddling a canoe down the last 2 km, one can see kingfishers diving or perched at the openings of their lengthy tunnel nests in the earth banks. The banks are thickly forested and there are bushbuck or waterbuck grazing on the grassy meadows adjoining the river, and one may perhaps encounter a leguaan or caracal (lynx) or even (in the early morning or evening) an otter.

This area is part of the Waters Meeting Nature Reserve, originally established as a forest reserve in 1897 to protect it from exploitation by farmers and boat builders. Various sections were later proclaimed as nature reserves in 1952 and 1985, and it now covers 4,247 hectares. But the best way to experience the river is by following the Kowie Canoe Trail, passing the Old Wreck, Windy Reach, Rabbit Rocks, Kob Hole, Black Rock, the Old Mill, the Reef, Fairy Glen and White Rock on the way to the four-room wooden chalet at Horseshoe Bend. This is a lovely spot, deeply shaded with white milkwood trees and containing a 12 km circular hiking route through the nature reserve, where one can encounter the creatures of the riverine forest. This is the best place to hear some of the sounds and glimpse a few of these wild creatures or their signs. Camping at the overnight shelter in the forest huts built for hikers and canoeists may be a frightening but also an exhilarating experience. Monkeys frequent the area and leopard tracks have been seen. There are still shy and secretive creatures around, like waterbuck, caracals, several mongoose species, bushpigs and porcupines, and one may hear the warning shouts of the chacma baboon, the cough-like bark of the bushbuck and the weird grunting, followed by a long-drawn-out creaking scream, of the tree hyrax (dassie), probably the most memorable of the bush night sounds.

* * *

The intermediate climatic position of the Kowie catchment area between the areas of western winter and eastern summer rainfall has created a rich floral region. The predominant vegetation of the area is what botanists call Albany Thicket, relatively impenetrable, woody, semi-succulent, thorny vegetation. It hosts a remarkable diversity of plants, especially succulents, bulbs and climbers, many endemic to the region, and has the widest range of plant forms found in any of South Africa's vegetation types.[21] Albany Thicket is more than 50 million years old and existed before grassland, savannah, karoo and perhaps even fynbos. Experts estimate that there are approximately 6,500 plant species in Albany Thicket, as well as an impressive number of animals, including 5 species of tortoise, 48 large mammals, 25 ungulates and 421 birds.[22]

There are wild fig trees and magnificent coral trees, which the British settlers used for roof shingles. In the forested valleys there are white ironwood, white stinkwood and yellowwood trees from which solid wheels were cut by the settlers. They are often draped with the long, grey lichen known as 'old man's beard'. There are wild olive trees, and at the bottom of the Waters Meeting Nature Reserve one can sit in the deep shade of the septee trees. White milkwood trees are common. One of the three white milkwood trees, *umqwashu* in isiXhosa, that have been declared national monuments is not too far away. This place, Emqwashini, is situated on the road to Alice from Peddie, and here in May 1835 the Mfengu affirmed their loyalty to the British king after being granted land in the area by the Cape governor, Sir Benjamin D'Urban. Once large enough to shelter thousands, today, having been struck by lightning and damaged in political protest, this milkwood is a sad, straggly reminder of its former size.

The riparian vegetation along the riverbanks contains representative examples of valley bushveld, including subtropical plants like the wild date palm, the leaves of which the British settlers used for making hats. There are Western Cape proteas and geraniums, tall candelabra-shaped euphorbias, bright aloes, cabbage trees, Cape chestnut trees covered with pink blossoms in spring, orange Cape honeysuckle attracting brilliant sunbirds, blue plumbagos, arum lilies, and species of prehistoric cycads. It is beautiful country which I associate with the colour orange, the colour of the bright orange and blue *Strelitzia reginae* crane flowers growing in the indigenous vegetation on the steep slopes of the riverbanks, the colour of aloes in flower, the blooms of the coral trees, as well as the traditional blankets and cosmetic paste on the faces of recently circumcised young Xhosa men.

The vegetation in the Kowie catchment area includes a cactus species which yields *itolofiya*, or prickly pears, small fruits with yellow-green skins. These are delicious to eat and were used by the many inhabitants of the area – Xhosa, Dutch and British – to make jam, chutney, syrup and a potent drink known as *iqhilika* by the Xhosa or *witblits* by the Afrikaners.[23] *Portulacaria afra*, a hardy plant with fleshy leaves and small pink flowers known locally as *spekboom*, grows widely and was the favourite food of the elephants that used to roam the area. The elephants have disappeared but the ancient order of cycads remains.

Millions of years ago the climate was warmer and wetter and the land covered in marshes and forests. Remains of the dinosaur *Paranthodon* were found nearby beside the Bushmans River in 1845. This was one of the earliest recognised dinosaur discoveries in the world and was certainly the first in South Africa.[24] One can still see the leguaan or water monitor lizard, which is reminiscent of these extraordinary creatures. Long ago there were sabre-toothed cats, bear-dogs, giant pigs, short-necked giraffes, and several different kinds of primeval elephants.

Before colonisation the Zuurveld was home to colourful birds and exotic wildlife including all Africa's big game – lion, rhinoceros and large herds of elephant and buffalo. There were zebra and many types of buck – steenbok, hartebeest, eland, springbok and oribi. Hippos swam in the waters of the Kowie River valley and wild boar and leopard were common. Early in the nineteenth century a visitor recorded that the 'close jungle on the banks ... of the Kowie abounds with elephants and buffalos and wood-antelopes [presumably bushbuck]'.[25] In 1813 the Rev. John Campbell wrote of 'a large elephant at the mouth of the Kowie River'.[26] He reported that in 1821 'elephants were very numerous and lions plentiful' in the river valley. In 1846 Captain Butler reported that 'the bush along the Kowie is full of game, not being yet deserted even by elephant and buffalo'.[27] Another visitor to the area in 1891 recorded frequent accounts of leopards being killed, herds of quagga running into hundreds, hippos, ostriches, bushpigs, red hares, Cape wild dogs and buffalo. All that is left are a few elephant remains, such as found at Salt Vlei in Port Alfred, and some tusks that were unearthed during the construction of the marina on the river.

All these animals were hunted by the Europeans, the Khoikhoi and the Xhosa, who surrounded their prey using assegais. John Campbell writes of the killing of a buffalo at the mouth of the Kowie River when he was there in 1815.[28] One authority maintains that the Bathurst district carried many 'of the usual plains game, mainly springboks, true quaggas, red hartebeest and elands which the 1820 settlers were to wipe out in the comparatively short time of about 20 years'.[29] Writing in 1835, Thomas Pringle observed that 'the forest-jungle which clothes the ravines that border the rivers of Albany, was at the time of this visit, still inhabited by some herds of buffaloes, and some species of the antelope and the hyena but the elephant had retreated since the arrival of the settlers'.[30]

It is said that the large pool lined with palms on Lushington farm was frequented by elephants and hippos, and although heavily hunted by all, hippos survived in the Kowie River for some years. There are reports of lions as late as 1846 when, on 28 February, one visited the residential part of Port Frances.[31] A small herd of buffaloes was reported in the Kowie bush on the outskirts of Bathurst in 1891.[32] An 80-year-old resident of Port Alfred remembers that his father, Gerald Stocks, used to 'hunt buffalo up the Kowie River'. The spotted hyena was once common but is now extinct in the Eastern Cape, as are lion, hunting dog, reedbuck, eland, red hartebeest, buffalo, warthog, elephant, hippopotamus, black rhinoceros and quagga.

This catalogue illustrates how, intent on the dominance and control of nature, we have pushed thousands of species to extinction. As Robert Macfarlane writes, 'the loss, after it is theirs, is ours. Wild animals, like wild places, are invaluable to us precisely because they are not us. They are uncompromisingly different. The paths they follow, the impulses that guide them, are of other orders ... seeing them you are made aware briefly of a world at work around and beside our own, a world operating in patterns and purposes that we do not share. These are creatures, you realise, that live by voices inaudible to you.'[33] The dominant concern today is the control and management of rivers, ignoring most of the wild species that depend on them. But we have much to learn from these wild creatures of the river. This includes the otter, intensely curious, tracing scent maps, moving easily between the water and the earth; the fish navigating back to their birth grounds, guided by memory and the stars; or the eagles riding the high thermals and scanning the earth below.

The iconic Cape Clawless Otter (*intini*) is my favourite river creature, one of the family immortalised in Ted Hughes's poem 'An Otter', which describes it as 'four-legged yet water-gifted'.[34] Our otters are mysterious, shy, but also curious and playful, with whiskered dog-like faces. 'She Comes Swimming' is a marvellous poem about sea otters by Isobel Dixon.[35] Otters are crepuscular, active in the early mornings and evenings, and I have spent many hours tracking them or sitting motionless on the riverbank hidden from view. Miriam Darlington writes of 'the carefully folded demeanour that otter-watching requires'.[36] In my own experience more is needed, not only absolute stillness, but pressing oneself into the smallest possible space, hidden from view in the reeds on the riverbank. Seeing otters is difficult as they are mud-coloured and their brown fur seems to merge with the shade of their background. The best way to discover their presence is to look carefully for their scat (droppings or spraint), which they leave as scent marks. These are usually full of fragments of crab shells or white mussels (their main diet) and are found in special toilet areas. I have seen one such place marked by thousands of white mussel shells hidden in the dense riverine vegetation.

Otters are very resourceful. They have been seen using rocks to break open crab and mussel shells. They are powerful swimmers, leaving a rippling wake, and this might be the first sign of an otter's presence. Or it could be the characteristic trail of bubbles the otter leaves as it swims beneath the surface. Jim Cambray described once seeing two otter pups riding on the back of their mother swimming in Blaauwkrantz pool.

* * *

There are still vervet monkeys, baboons, jackals, ratels (honey badgers), genets with their intricately patterned tails, and even leopards in the Kowie River bush. Very recently the pineapple farmer Fred Tyson saw a leopard on the banks of the Kowie where it winds through a very wild and hilly landscape. He said that otters were once more plentiful on his Langholm farm, but they 'used to steal chickens and so the workers killed them'.[37] In many places there are signs of bushpigs rooting quite deeply, and warthogs digging through the rich earth. The marks of bushbuck and kudu are everywhere, and the delicate footprints of the secretive blue duiker are unmistakable.

All of these animals are also found in nearby river valleys like the Kariega, the Kasouga, the Fish, the Bushmans and the Kap. The name Kasouga for the river between Port Alfred and Kenton-on-Sea is of Gonaqua Khoikhoi origin and is believed to mean 'full of leopards'. Leopards are secretive and nocturnal so they are very seldom seen. They are now protected, but a large one weighing 76 kg was 'accidentally' shot along the Kowie River in 1996. Mike Powell, the manager of the Waters Meeting Nature Reserve, wrote of a leopard he named Rocky who 'has been leaving spoor all over the reserve and often in neighbouring farms. He/she is thought to have probably been responsible for at least three sheep kills.'[38] A keen conservationist, Powell liked to think of Rocky the leopard as well as the Eastern Cape Rocky (the freshwater fish threatened with extinction that is found in the Kowie River) as two key indicator species. He established a fund in the name of Rocky to save this leopard and others, and to provide compensation to farmers whose stock has been killed by them.

There used to be a total of 36 different fish species in the Kowie estuary. Recreational rather than subsistence fishing is still widely practised, though. In 2004 the annual yield of fish from the estuary was relatively low, being only some 16,240 fish or 5.99 tons. Recreational anglers caught 69 per cent of the catch, mainly three species, Cape Stumpnose, Spotted Grunter and Dusky Kob. Estuary-dependent marine migrant species dominate most of the catch from the Kowie estuary. These are species which breed at sea and enter the estuary as juveniles to feed and grow. The protection of critical habitats on the estuary has often been recommended. According to a marine scientist, 'in terms of catch numbers Cape Stumpnose is the most important fish species on the estuary and to protect them the conservation of zostera (Cape sea grass) beds should be given priority. Serious threats to the zostera beds include siltation of the estuary.'[39]

Today there are only five indigenous freshwater fish species in the river systems between the Bushmans and the Great Fish rivers, according to Jim Cambray. He mentioned the Chubbyhead Barb as well as the Goldie Barb as occurring in the Kowie River. The part of the river running through Langholm farm contains many freshwater mullet, locally called 'springers'. According to both Jim Cambray and local resident Ronnie Slaughter, a local form of fishing for mullet has been developed using a Spanish reed for a rod, a porcupine quill for a float, and termites (white ants) as bait.

Some years ago the ecological community recorded on the Kowie estuary included 11 species of frogs, 24 species of reptiles, 93 species of birds and 31 species of mammals. There are also terrapins or turtles and eels which breed in the ocean off Madagascar. The young, leaf-like eels (known as *leptocephali*) float on the currents along the African coast. They turn into small eels, which you can see through, and so are known as 'glass eels'. They enter the rivers mainly on summer nights on high spring tides when the river is flowing strongly. These anguillid eels use the estuaries as a conduit between the sea and the river. They swim upstream during migration and return along the same path on their way to the marine environment where spawning occurs. Their journey inspired two different ecologists writing at different times, at opposite ends of the world and unknown to each other, Rachel Carson and Jim Cambray.

The Kowie catchment area is exceptionally rich in birdlife, with more than 400 species having been recorded since 1960 in the Eastern Cape, 5 km inland from the shoreline as well as on the shore itself. According to Biff Todd, between 1973 and 1982, 93 species of water-associated birds were recorded in the Kowie and Bathurst districts, including 35 species of waders, which frequent the mud flats of the estuary exposed at low tide.[40] In the forested riverbanks one may glimpse the dramatic black-and-yellow plumage of the Forest Weaver, and hear the liquid notes of the Black-headed Oriole, as well as the plaintive voice of the Grey-headed Bush Shrike and the tantalising hoot of the shy and exquisite Narina Trogon. Black-headed Herons stand patiently fishing in the shallows, only revealing their massive wings in ponderous flight. While the cry of the African Fish Eagle used to be more common than it is now, one may still experience a dramatic river sighting as, with distinctive shining white breast, curved beak and big wingspan, one drops, crashing feet first into the water, throwing up a curtain of spray, and then flying off with a silver fish in its talons.

The Kowie River also hosts several migrant waders from the northern hemisphere, like the Greenshank. Other winter visitors include small groups of Black Storks and occasionally Ospreys. Cape and White-breasted Cormorants are common, as are various kinds of terns. All five varieties of kingfisher have been seen on the river, with the Pied, the most common, hovering in perfect balance, the Giant watchful from a branch overhanging the water, and the Half-collared and Malachite providing flashes of turquoise. The Brown-hooded Kingfisher is a striking-looking bird with its spear-like scarlet beak and azure coloration of its tail. It is a dryland kingfisher, and large grasshoppers and locusts are among its favourite food items.

In the early morning the forested banks of the Kowie are alive with birdsong. There are occasional glimpses of the shy African Finfoot gliding along low in the water and sunbirds feeding on the aloes during the winter months. Yellow Weavers breed in the reedbeds of the upper reaches and flocks of Egyptian Geese feed in the lands adjacent to the riverbanks.

The thick river vegetation shelters more retiring species such as the Black-headed Night Heron and Black Ducks. Martial Eagles still occur in the area, and for years the large, untidy nest of a Crowned Eagle was visible from the viewing site at the top of the horseshoe in the Kowie Forest Reserve. Crowned Eagles practise what has been termed 'the Cain and Abel syndrome' whereby firstborn chicks kill their younger siblings. We are not sure why, especially as African Fish Eagles rear two or three chicks in harmony. On the banks of the Lushington River, near its confluence with the Kowie, there used to be a large, domed nest of the 'lightning bird' or Hamerkop, which is said, in Xhosa tradition, to bring good luck. The Giant Eagle Owl has also been seen and the exquisite little Barred Owl, long thought to be extinct in the area, was recently sighted. Little Egrets, Grey Herons and Water Thick-knees (dikkop) loiter in the shallows and the large sandbanks provide nesting for swifts, while Cape, Reed and White-breasted Cormorants are visible on perches along the riverbanks soaking up the sun and preening. The salt marshes are frequented by spoonbills, plovers and Yellow-billed Ducks. At the river mouth African Black Oystercatchers pick their way among the mussel beds at low tide, with the turnstones and plovers. Several varieties of tern frequent this spot, including the Arctic Tern, which covers the globe in its migratory patterns, and far out to sea one may see Cape Gannets plunge-diving.

Near the river mouth there used to be a salt marsh, a type of wetland known locally as the 'flats', fringing the estuarine water surface. These mud flats, or salt marshes, looked like those on the west bank of the Fish and Keiskamma rivers, rich-smelling with beautiful shades of pink and green fleshy plants. The whole area contained a diverse population of worms, prawns, crabs and fish as well as wading birds – particularly the Palaearctic migrants – during low tides. The adjacent lagoon contained large kob and in the evening one could watch Spotted Grunter feeding with their tails waving vertically in the air, breaking the still, grey surface.

This wetland was sometimes described as a 'dead swamp' by locals. Its loss during the construction of the marina is part of a larger pattern of destruction. It is estimated that by 1996 more than half of all South Africa's wetlands had already been destroyed or otherwise lost. The main threats are not only artificial breaching for marina developments, but water abstraction and dam construction, which obviously reduce the amount and seasonal patterns of fresh water flowing into an estuary, as well as eutrophication caused by the run-off of nutrients from agriculture, septic tanks, malfunctioning sewage treatment plants and habitat loss. The crucial question is whether the Kowie is enough of what T.S. Eliot called a 'strong brown god'[41] to withstand these threats.

The social history of the river

Historians now generally define the catchment area of the Kowie River as the Zuurveld, bounded by the Zuurberg and Fish River mountain chains in the north, the Fish River in the east, the Sundays River in the west, and the Indian Ocean to the south. However, during the period 1770–1812 'contemporaries also referred to the Zuurveld in the more restricted sense as the area between the Boesmans and the Fish Rivers'.[42] In 1778 Governor Van Plettenberg persuaded some imiDange chiefs to recognise the boundary of the colony as the upper reaches of the Great Fish River and the Boesmans River Mountains. Jeff Peires points out that 'it was not a solemn treaty with all the Xhosa chiefs along the Great Fish River'.[43] Two years later the Council of Policy proclaimed the Fish River along its entire length as the boundary.

The Dutch word *zuurveld*, the name for the catchment area of the Kowie, refers to the prevalent grass type in the area, meaning 'the land of sour grasses'. Being of high acidity, the soil produces grass which is harmful, even fatal, to cattle in autumn and winter. The main characteristic of 'sourveld' is that its 'nutritive value and palatability decreases as it matures. In the spring and early summer its food value is high and the grass is of great importance to the herdsmen. But it can only be fully utilised for about four months in the year before its food value becomes depleted and it loses its palatability. "Sweetveld" is therefore of particular importance as winter grazing if cattle are to maintain condition.'[44] Consequently the Zuurveld was only suitable as pasture during the summer months, though the sweetveld of the river valleys provided good grazing throughout the year. All the early inhabitants of the area, Khoikhoi, Dutch and Xhosa, needed therefore to move their herds of cattle between seasonal pastures, alternating summer grazing on the sourveld with winter grazing on the sweetveld.

* * *

The original inhabitants of the Zuurveld were Khoikhoi pastoralists, who moved about the area seasonally in search of water and grazing. Their prior inhabitation has been shown conclusively by the written accounts of all the early European travellers who passed through the region in the eighteenth century. When Ensign Beutler visited the Eastern Cape in 1752 he found the Kowie area was inhabited by Khoikhoi people identified as the Gonaqua. They were already in the process of intermarrying with and being absorbed by the neighbouring Xhosa into what would become known as the Gqunukhwebe chiefdom. Beutler observed that 'the clothing and way of life' of the Xhosa and the Gonaqua 'are similar and they intermarry without differentiation'. As has been observed, 'the longevity of their interaction is illustrated by the wholehearted adoption of Khoisan clicks into isiXhosa'.[45] In this way the Zuurveld became a site of intense social interaction and 'ethnic ambiguity'.[46]

Khoikhoi was a very fluid social and political category: groups constantly broke up and amalgamated over time. Between about 1752 and 1772 the dominant political figure in the Zuurveld was the Hoengiqua chief known to the Dutch as Ruyter. He was not a chief by birth but gathered together numbers of followers and was respected by the Xhosa as well as by the Dutch. According to the traveller Colonel Robert Gordon, who came across the clan in the vicinity of what is now Kenton, Ruyter's people claimed sovereignty over the Zuurveld between the Sundays and the Fish rivers.[47]

Much of the land the Khoikhoi occupied was taken from them by incoming trekboers. From about 1770 these semi-nomadic Dutch farmers, whom the English missionary Stephen Kay referred to disparagingly as 'white barbarians', began to settle in the Zuurveld, drawn to its well-watered grazing lands and fertile soil. 'In defiance of the colonial regulations, they had taken possession of the choicest spots they could find beyond the nominal boundary – then the Gamtoos river.'[48] They raided the livestock of the Khoikhoi, burnt down their dwellings and drove them off the land. Khoikhoi were also attacked by the Xhosa under Rharhabe, who had moved westwards over the Kei River.

By the end of the century the Khoikhoi had lost most of their land to European colonists, large numbers had died of newly introduced diseases such as smallpox, and many were forced into the service of the colonists either as labourers or as soldiers. The missionary John Philip wrote, 'The Hottentots are acknowledged to be a free people but labour is every day becoming scarcer, and the colonists are resolved to indemnify themselves for the loss of the slave trade by reducing the Hottentots to a condition of slavery the more shocking and oppressive.'[49] One of the ironies of history is that Khoikhoi soldiers played a decisive role in the defeat of the Xhosa in the Battle of Grahamstown in 1819 and in the expulsion of the Xhosa from the Zuurveld in 1811–12. Their vulnerability had turned them into collaborators with the colonists.

* * *

Land and water are crucial to understanding the history of the area. The Kowie River was at the centre of the Xhosa world for the thousands living in the Zuurveld on the eastern frontier of the colony. The Xhosa lived in dispersed settlements, with each chiefdom occupying a particular river valley. According to Jeff Peires, 'It was the water not the land which determined the pattern of human settlement. Ideally each chiefdom had its own river and each sub-chiefdom had its own tributary ... there was no latitude for doubt in the matter of access to water. Only the people of the community and their cattle had the right to drink the water of their own particular stream. Thus nearly all Xhosa place-names are the names of rivers.'[50]

It seems fairly certain that, at least by 1778, the Gqunukhwebe under Chief Tshaka occupied the Kowie River valley and the area as far west as the Bushmans River. They had lived longer in the Zuurveld than the other Xhosa groups and had long intermarried with the Khoikhoi. When Colonel Gordon visited the Zuurveld in 1778 he met with several Xhosa chiefs who had crossed the Keiskamma after 1752. A number were living west of the Bushmans River and one as far as the Zwartkops River. In 1798 the British official John Barrow described encountering 'a prodigious number of Kaffers with their cattle, belonging, as they told us, to a powerful chief named Congo [Chungwa, the son of Tshaka]'.[51] 'Two officials sent in 1797 to visit the Zuurveld and report on conditions, met with a number of Xhosa chiefs living near the coast, close to the Bushmans and Kariega rivers.'[52] These encounters completely refute the colonial myth that white and black arrived in the empty land of the Zuurveld simultaneously in the late eighteenth century.

At this time the Kowie River catchment area was dotted with Xhosa homesteads containing clusters of beehive-shaped dwellings with clay walls and thatched roofs, thorn-fenced enclosures of cattle with elaborately shaped horns, and gardens of maize, sorghum, pumpkins and melons. These horned cattle were the fulcrum of Xhosa social and spiritual life, and their meat and milk were the principal means of subsistence. The Xhosa had twenty-five names to describe different cattle-skin patterns and colours, and seven different names for the shapes of their horns. 'The Xhosa lived in an intensely personal environment. He was part of it and he felt at home in it.'[53]

But by 1779 armed clashes began between the Dutch and Xhosa chiefdoms such as the Gqunukhwebe and Ndlambe in the area between the Sundays and Fish rivers. Fundamentally, these were struggles for access to and control of pasture and water. The tension was exacerbated by conflicting views about both land and identity. The colonists thought of occupation as conferring an exclusive right on individuals, whereas the Xhosa saw land as communal property, the boundaries of which were very loosely defined. Conflict was also informed by different understandings of society and identity. 'Xhosa society was basically an open one which, through intermarriage and other means, incorporated and eventually integrated non-Nguni speakers. There is evidence that Xhosa were inclined to incorporate the colonists in the same way.'[54] In sharp contrast to this egalitarian inclusivity, the colonisers claimed a dominant and exclusive identity.

* * *

The armed clashes which marked the years of conflict were intermittent and involved episodic cattle raids and skirmishes rather than dramatic confrontations between armed protagonists. But the stakes were high and many lives were lost. It was a conflict which extended in a Hundred Years War from 1779 (the outbreak of the first war) to 1878 (the conclusion of the ninth and last). These are usually described as 'frontier wars' or, more recently, as 'wars of dispossession'. The first two clashes took place between the Dutch and the Xhosa, but during later clashes the British colonial forces gradually forced the Xhosa back across the Kowie, then the Fish, and finally across the Keiskamma and the Kei, almost to the site of what is now Mthatha.

The historian Julie Wells argues that the Xhosa tactics over this period 'are best described as a form of harassment, rather than "warfare"'.[55] It was fundamentally a sustained guerrilla struggle. To the Xhosa the Zuurveld was theirs by birthright, conquest or purchase long before whites appeared in the area. The Gqunukhwebe Xhosa, in particular, insisted that they had bought the land along the coast between the Kowie and the Fish rivers from the Hoengiqua chief Ruyter for 800 head of cattle, and refused to renounce their claim.[56]

The Kowie was the scene of some of the earliest armed encounters. After the first of these clashes, Commandant Adriaan van Jaarsveld wrote in his diary on 17 July 1781 that he attacked the Xhosa 'lying at the Thouhie on this side of Great Fish River, but from the number of forests could kill very few, but we also captured part of their cattle to the number of 2,000 and returned'. The second (1793) and third (1799–1803) wars were actually won by the Xhosa, who pushed as far west as Plettenberg Bay.[57]

Throughout the late 1780s and 1790s increasing numbers of Xhosa moved west into the Zuurveld, largely following the attempts by the Xhosa chiefs Ndlambe and Ngqika to extend their power in the region. In 1799 the first major confrontation between Xhosa and Dutch occurred, when Ndlambe moved with large numbers of his followers into the Zuurveld, joining his brother who was already living there. As Sir Andries Stockenström later recalled, 'the Colonists were driven out of the Zuurveld, their houses burnt, many lives lost, and the Kaffirs settled down between the Bushman and Sundays rivers, and even to the westward of the latter'. A meeting between Ndlambe and the colonial official Jacob Cuyler in 1808 'revealed that the amaNdlambe were in full occupation and control of the Zuurveld, right up to Algoa Bay in the west, and extending northward into the interior mountains'.[58]

While the Xhosa consistently fought against European encroachment, Ndlambe tried hard to persuade the colonial authorities that his claim to the Zuurveld was legitimate. In 1810 he met Anders Stockenström, the landdrost of Graaff-Reinet, whose son Andries described the encounter in this way: 'The Kaffir Chief received us with civility, but expressed much annoyance at being so repeatedly disturbed in the peaceful possession of land, which he again protested he had purchased and paid for. He said it had cost him 800 oxen, with great emphasis, backed by the Councillors, describing the colour, shape of the horns, etc. of many of the cattle thus paid.'[59]

Despite these efforts to make peace, from at least 1812 the area of the Zuurveld centred on the Kowie River became a theatre of guerrilla warfare involving military patrols and cattle raiding.[60] In most of these clashes the thickly forested banks of rivers like the Kowie and the Fish were crucial to the Xhosa in providing cover, making ambush possible and cavalry movement difficult. This would, however, be of no avail at the decisive Battle of Grahamstown in 1819.

* * *

Although European colonists only entered the Zuurveld in significant numbers in the late eighteenth century, the region had been visited and observed by Europeans for much longer. There may well have been Khoikhoi watching as the Portuguese seafaring explorers, including

Vasco da Gama, sailed past the Kowie on their way to the east. Any watchers from the Kowie mouth would have been the light, wiry, yellow-skinned people whom the colonists called *Strandlopers* (beach walkers). They seem to have lived for most of the year on the beaches, collecting mussels and other shellfish, eating seals and the occasional beached whale. The only signs that remain of these original inhabitants are the piles of shell fragments, or middens, found in the shifting sand dunes on the desolate, windy coast to the east and west of the Kowie River mouth.

According to the historian Eric Axelson, Bartolomeu Dias passed the Kowie in 1488, sailing as far as the Keiskamma River, where he turned back. While there is controversy about whether the early Portuguese explorers visited the Kowie, new evidence is emerging about contact between China and Africa in the fifteenth century, sixty years before the Portuguese. Chinese maps of the period depict the coasts of east, south and west Africa so clearly 'that there cannot be a shred of doubt that it was charted by someone who had sailed around the Cape'.[61] From the sixteenth to the eighteenth century, castaways and perhaps pirates may also have spent time at the Kowie River mouth. The old customs house, which once stood in the dense bush of the east bank of the Kowie River, was built in 1826 on the site of an earlier structure thought by local people to belong to Portuguese pirates.[62]

Shipwrecks were frequent along this coast, and Portuguese, English and Dutch castaways must have passed the Kowie on their arduous journey to either Mozambique or Cape Town, confronting the hardships of flooded rivers, locals whose languages they did not speak, starvation and especially thirst. Many shipwrecked survivors died of dehydration or were reduced to drinking their own urine or, in the case of the survivors of the *São João Baptista*, which sank near the Fish River mouth in 1622, eating their companions, who smelt 'most excellently like pork'.[63]

The site of the wreck of the *São João Baptista* is disputed, but it is known that survivors of the East Indiaman *Johanna* passed this way in 1683. However, the most pathetic of these early European travellers who crossed the Kowie must surely have been the small group of survivors of the *Grosvenor*, which ran ashore on the Pondoland coast in 1782. Six of them crossed the Kowie and made their way to the Zwartkops River further west. They were clearly given a safe passage by the local people. The group included William Hubberley, who crossed the Kowie on 7 November 1782. He wrote, 'I then crossed a small river, and found water but few shellfish on account of the shore being for the most part sandy.'[64] Hubberley was one of the lucky ones in that he made it to the Cape and back to Europe, but he experienced a gruelling journey. He witnessed the death of his two companions: one was driven into the Fish River and stoned until he drowned and the other beaten to death by Xhosa men. Hubberley himself became a skeleton, living on shellfish and 'hottentot figs'. However, he experienced kindness from some of the local Xhosa people in the area of the Kowie, stayed with them for three days and was given some boiled meat and on another occasion some milk, which 'was the only food they had for themselves'. While some Xhosa were 'very friendly', others threw stones and sticks at him. He offended one Xhosa group by relieving himself in the cattle byre.[65]

Apart from castaways, the first recorded Europeans in the area of the Kowie River were hunters and traders. From roughly the middle of the eighteenth century there were numerous hunting and trading expeditions to the Eastern Cape, mainly involving elephant hunters in search of ivory. This was also a valuable item of trade with the Xhosa. Hendrik Swellengrebel, son of the Dutch governor of the same name, journeyed to the area in the late 1770s and mentioned in his journal the 'Thouhie' river, which seems to be a reference to the Kowie. The Dutch soldier and explorer Robert Gordon and the Swedish botanist Anders Sparrman have given us rich observations of the birds, animals and people of the Zuurveld area. During the early years of British rule at the Cape, explorers like Henry Lichtenstein and officials like John Barrow left vivid accounts of visiting the Kowie area.

The 1752 expedition led by Ensign August Beutler was the first serious attempt by the Cape government to ascertain the potentialities of the region. It was launched on a large scale, involving seventy-one people initially, but with 'interpreters and other Hottentots' this increased to about a hundred. They travelled more than three thousand kilometres over nine months mainly along the eastern coast and detoured some distance inland 'because of the numerous kloofs and woods that lay in our way'. During their journey they rested on the banks of what they called the Buffelsbosch River, which, it is said, was the Kowie. Beutler described the water of this river as 'completely muddy and most unpleasant to drink'.[66] The party travelled extensively through what would become the Zuurveld and in May 1752 Beutler met the Hoengiqua chief, Captain Ruyter, who accompanied him as far as the Keiskamma River. He described the Khoikhoi unflatteringly as 'stupid' and 'idle'; 'they would rather die of hunger than work', though it seems these comments were reserved for the men, for he went on to say, 'All this [cooking and beer-making] as well as tending the land and sowing is the work of women, as the men, apart from milking the cows ... do nothing else but herd the cattle, hunt and amuse themselves while they treat their women no better than slaves.'[67] Nevertheless, he was impressed by the extensive botanical knowledge of the Khoikhoi.

When Robert Gordon set out in 1777 with his Khoikhoi guide to travel along the coast from the mouth of the Fish to the Sundays, he encountered dense bush filled with elephants and buffalo and failed to find a path for his wagon. He did discover the remains of Bartolomeu Dias's cross on a rocky outcrop called Kwaaihoek not very far from the Kowie. In January 1778, near the mouth of the Bushmans River, Gordon found the elderly chief Ruyter. He described him as a man 'with a polite manner and very pleasing appearance ... He was very pleased when I informed him that my great chief [the Dutch governor Van Plettenberg] liked him very much because he had always been a good chief.'[68] Ruyter was visited by several travellers, among them Swellengrebel, the Scottish plant collector William Paterson and the Swedish botanist Sparrman. Sparrman described Ruyter as 'cruel' but also 'a true and faithful ally', a buffer between the Xhosa and the colonists.

One of the most colourful of the early travellers was François Le Vaillant, South Africa's Audubon. With his silver-buckled shoes, large elegant hat adorned with ostrich feathers, and colourful coat and waist-coat, this young French explorer visited the Cape from 1780 until 1784 and undertook two major trips of exploration, one to the eastern limits of the Cape Colony. He described and drew 284 species of birds and in many cases added notes on their habits, publishing several volumes of travel writing and six volumes on the birds of Africa. On much of his travels he was accompanied by his pet baboon, Kees, who rode on the back of one of the dogs when he tired.

Near the Great Fish River in 1782, Le Vaillant encountered some Xhosa, whom he described as 'not naturally cruel, living like the other natives of this part of Africa, on the simple produce of their flocks, their nourishment milk and skins their clothing; peaceful by nature, warriors only from necessity; and by no means a nation whose name ought to inspire horror'.[69] In his opinion the Xhosa 'are in general harmless and peaceable, but being continually pillaged, harassed, nay often murdered by the whites, they are obliged to take up arms in their own defence'.[70]

It is not certain if Le Vaillant reached the Kowie. Near the Sundays River he seems to have turned northwards. 'On the banks of the Zwartkops River he met a group of Khoi who advised him not to go eastwards across the Bushmans River because of marauding bands of Kaffirs who had their haunts there.'[71] In this region he met a beautiful young Khoikhoi woman of the Gonaqua people, whom he called Narina, after whom the bird Narina Trogon is named. His account of his travels devotes much attention to his dalliance with this fair maiden.

With his sensibility shaped by Jean-Jacques Rousseau, the flamboyant Le Vaillant could not have been more different from John Barrow, the British governor's private secretary, who was sent in 1797 as a young man of 33 to obtain first-hand information about the eastern frontier and its people for the new administration, shortly after Britain had seized the Cape from the Dutch. Barrow's published account of his journey reveals keen powers of observation of the landscape and a lively sympathy for the indigenous people. He travelled from the mouth of the Kowie River to the mouth of the Great Fish and did so 'with great difficulty', crossing the deep valley of the Kowie somewhere between its confluence with the Blaauwkrantz to the north and with the Torrens (also called the Lushington) to the south.[72] He wrote, 'a more difficult and dreadful place was certainly never attempted by wheel-carriages'.[73]

The Xhosa men Barrow encountered in the area 'were the finest figures I ever beheld: they were tall, robust and muscular; their habits of life had induced a firmness of carriage and an open, manly manner, which, added to the good nature that overspread their features, showed them at once to be equally unconscious of fear, suspicion and treachery'.[74] Barrow described the Khoikhoi as 'a mild, quiet and timid people; perfectly harmless, honest, faithful, and though extremely phlegmatic, they are kind and affectionate to each other'.[75] He was indignant about the cruelty to which they were subjected by some Dutch farmers, 'which included a Hottentot bound to a tree made to cut a piece of flesh out of his thigh and eat it'.[76] He described their lives as 'a state of existence to which that of slavery might bear the comparison of happiness'.[77]

In Barrow's opinion, the Zuurveld was 'the most beautiful division in the whole district', 'well wooded and watered' with 'a great depth of good soil'. He reported: 'The great chasms towards the sea-coast, that are filled with thickets, abound in elephants and buffalos, and in the Great Fish River occasionally, a few of the hippopotamus.'[78] Elephants were found in large herds, and there were also leopards and hyenas. However, he lamented that 'the well-clothed plains of Zuur Veldt, when inhabited by the Dutch, abounded with a variety of game, especially of the antelope tribe; but since the arrival of the Kaffers they have mostly been destroyed or chased into some other part of the country'.[79] He wrote that the area 'is now [1798] exclusively in the possession of the Kaffers, from whom, indeed, it was originally taken forcibly by the boors'.[80]

Barrow delighted in the 'lofty' and 'beautiful' yellowwood trees, as well as the 'euphorbia, [which] throwing out a number of naked arms from a straight trunk thirty or forty feet high, held a distinguished place among the shrubbery'. But his favourite was the coral tree (*Erythrina caffra*), which attracted 'numbers of beautiful birds, such as small parakeets, touracos, woodpeckers and others'.[81]

After the British retook the Cape in 1806, having given it back to the Dutch in 1802, Colonel Richard Collins was, like Barrow, sent on a tour of the Eastern Cape by the new British government in 1809 to report on the situation there. He recommended that the land near the Great Fish River be annexed to the colony and that settlers placed there in the buffer zone. He also thought of establishing a harbour in the area and wrote, 'The river Guasouwga [presumably the Kasouga] flowing between the Kowie and Kareegha is a fine stream, that can cover a quantity of excellent lands. It falls into the sea, at a place that affords a good landing.'[82] Collins's recommendations were in many respects to be accepted and carried out by the British government, as we shall see.

One should not underestimate the perseverance of these early travellers. Travelling was uncomfortable and slow, and what with the encumbrance of wagons, oxen and difficult terrain, they sometimes covered only six or seven miles in a day. 'A long journey in the Africa of [that] day, without any companion or maps or knowledge of the country or of native languages, was a hazardous undertaking.'[83] But these early travellers did have 'companions', guides and interpreters. As William Dicey has pointed out in his wonderful account of the Orange River in *Borderline*, travellers like Sparrman, Barrow and Le Vaillant were all 'accompanied on their pioneering endeavours by Khoisan and Baster servants, guides and sometimes companions. Indeed, these people now lost in nameless oblivion were crucial to the success of the expeditions, given their knowledge of the terrain, their skill in handling oxen and their ability to communicate with local tribes.'[84]

One such traveller was William Burchell, who visited the Kowie in 1813 on his five-year-long journey with his fifty reference books, his flute, his faithful dog Wantrouw and many Khoikhoi servants. He took back with him to England some sixty thousand natural history specimens, mostly botanical and animal, several of them from the Kowie area. He spent time here in September 1813 and recommended European settlement in the area. He thought that 'perhaps the best situation for a town might be on the Kowie River, somewhere above the influence of the saltwater, as boats might advance a considerable way up it, if it should prove practicable to pass the bar at its mouth'.[85] Burchell collected over eight hundred specimens in the area bounded by Kaffir Drift on the Fish River and the Kasouga River. He went as far east as the mouth of the Fish River and has left us lyrical descriptions and delicate drawings and paintings.[86]

In the same year as Burchell's visit, the Rev. John Campbell, travelling superintendent of the London Missionary Society, while searching for a site on which to build his mission, described the Kowie as having 'a formidable aspect'.[87] He recorded that his wagons entered the Kowie at a point where it was about a quarter of a mile wide, about 600 yards from the river mouth. The backs of the oxen were under water, and the party had to swim for part of the distance. From the left bank they ascended a steep elephant path through the trees, and had to cut branches to allow the passage of their wagons. He too collected a wagonload of exotic specimens, including the skull of a rhino, which he imagined to be a unicorn.

Another early traveller to the Kowie was George Thompson, a Cape Town merchant and explorer, who came here in 1823 with his 'Hottentot guide'. He was full of praise for both the country and its inhabitants. He described the Xhosa as 'an honest, humane and civilised race' and spoke about the 'long oppressed and neglected Hottentots'. He presented the Zuurveld as 'a rich and smiling scene'. He found 'luxuriant woods and copses of ever-greens, in the disposal of which the wanton hand of Nature seemed to have rivalled the most tasteful efforts of art'.[88] The Lower Albany countryside was 'the most beautiful and pleasing I have ever seen in Africa'.[89] Thompson argued for clearing the sandbar at the mouth of the Kowie and developing it into a port. He quoted a report by Commander Nourse to the governor of 17 October 1823, saying, 'I think it would be worth the experiment to make the course straight from the bar to the straighter and deeper part of the river.' He added: 'Although Algoa Bay had hitherto been considered as the port of the new settlement, its distance from the frontier renders it less eligible than Port Frances at the Kowie river mouth, which is the next port to the eastward and which river flows through the heart of the district of Albany.'[90]

* * *

In geological time the history I have described here concerns very recent events. For millions of years the Kowie River was wild and diverse. But in the last 150 years there have been two assaults on the ecological integrity of the river: a harbour and a marina, both of which justified destruction in the name of 'development'. But both were only possible because of a battle fought in the vicinity of the Kowie in 1819, a battle which changed the course of South African history.

While today the waters of the Kowie River vary between a sky blue, with streaks of brown reflecting the mud banks, or green where the water is deep, there was a time when a stretch of its main tributary, the Blaauwkrantz, was red with blood. This was the river some locals term the Kowie Ditch, which flows through Grahamstown, and the blood was that of some of the thousand Xhosa warriors killed in the battle that took place in the vicinity in 1819. Many of the wounded crawled away from the fighting, trying to stop the bleeding from bullet holes with tufts of grass, and hid in the waters of the Kowie tributary. The site is now known by the Xhosa as *Egazini*, 'the place of blood'. It is widely acknowledged by historians that this event was a turning point in South African history. It was also decisive in the history of the Kowie River.

* * *

In 2005, on 22 April, dressed in black, I flew from Johannesburg to attend a re-enactment of this battle. This took place on the site where the Xhosa assembled below the pine-covered hill known to them as *intaba izono* (the mountain of danger) and to whites as Makana's Kop. It was a colourful and noisy scene: some people were dressed in red coats to represent the British colonial army, while others in loincloths with cowhide shields, spears, and fake leopard skins, took the part of Xhosa warriors. A four-pounder cannon, muskets, kudu horns and drums provided the props of war. Starting with a procession of drum majorettes from a local school to the viewing site overlooking the town, the occasion had a festive atmosphere. To the schoolchildren, who seemed to constitute the majority of the watching crowd, it was an occasion of fun and hilarity rather than one of mourning. My black clothing was somewhat inappropriate. Scant attention was paid to the speeches of the dignitaries such as Prince Jongolo from the AmaNdlambe Traditional Council. There was little sense of the tragic significance of the event being commemorated: 'tragic' in terms of the scale of the Xhosa casualties, 'significant' in the sense of its historical consequences.

This was an event of which I had been totally ignorant, despite having studied history at school in Grahamstown and at Rhodes University. At that time the research of historians such as Jeff Peires, Tim Keegan, Clifton Crais, Julie Wells and Martin Legassick had not been published. The great Xhosa leader Makhanda was then still demonised by many historians as a charlatan, witchdoctor and religious fanatic, and his army as an 'aggressive horde' of 'howling Kaffir warriors'.

Since then, a tendency to simplify and even distort the battle has further obscured our understanding. For example, an article in the December 1979 issue of the underground ANC journal, *Sechaba*, stated: 'The defeat at Grahamstown on the morning of 23rd April 1819 does not suggest the weakness of our people, neither does it point to the paucity of the strategy and tactics employed by Makhanda; instead it points to the dazzling bravery of our people who with only spears in hand took the fort at Grahamstown by such a storm that a countless number of settlers were left lifeless, several hundred mortally wounded. The resultant driving away of Makhanda and Ndlambe's forces, therefore, was an event made possible only by the fact that the British wielded superior weapons. The advantage the British enjoyed failed, however, to vanquish the indomitable spirit of Makhanda and the people whom he welded into an indestructible unity, his men displayed tremendous courage, bravery and unity of action as well as of purpose.'[1] But as I have since discovered, the roots of the Battle of Grahamstown lay not in the personality of one man, but in the claim of the Xhosa to their land.

The battle must have been terrifying for all the inhabitants of the straggly little town of Grahamstown, as well as for the British and Xhosa fighters and the thousands of Xhosa women and children watching from the hilltops. Chief Ndlambe's army, numbering about ten thousand, was led by the prophet-warrior Makhanda, along with other Xhosa chiefs such as Mdushane, son of Ndlambe, and Phato, son of the deceased Chief Chungwa.

According to the account of the British commander, Colonel Willshire, 'About half past one o'clock on 22nd April, the Kaffirs amounting to 6,000 strong, made a most determined ... attack upon the town. The Xhosa charged down the hill, two columns making for the square, the third moving out towards the barracks in the flanking movement so characteristic of traditional warfare. As they ran they broke up into little knots of warriors, rendering the cannon initially ineffective. They got within 30 yards or so of the soldiers, their spears broken off for close combat, but they could not sustain their momentum in the face of the steady fire of disciplined troops. Khoi marksmen picked off the Xhosa leaders, but what really halted the charge was the nature of the weapons which they faced. While kneeling and ducking in front of the troops, the right hand was always raised with the assegai but their fear of looking at the fire prevented them from throwing as often or as correctly as they otherwise would have done. On seeing a flash they immediately placed the left arm with the karoos [bullock's hide] before their eyes.'[2]

Willshire commanded a force of 532 men and two guns. Initially he ordered his men to retreat back across the Kowie River tributary to take shelter around the artillery. Once the Xhosa were within range, they started firing with their 270 muskets and cannons. The Xhosa were armed only with short stabbing-spears. As the soldier Charles Lennox Stretch described the British fire, their 'field pieces were loaded with shrapnel shells, which with the destructive fire of the musketry, every shot of which was deadly, opened spaces like streets in the courageously advancing masses, with their wild war cries and they were literally mowed down, while their showers of assegais fell short or ineffective'.[3]

Finally the Xhosa retreated, repelled by the arrival of a group of Khoikhoi under Hendrik Bosak, and 'many of them died in the waters of the Kowie ditch'.[4] The river 'flowed red from the blood of the dead who had fallen atop one another there, and from the wounded who tried to hide among the grasses and slowly bled to death'.[5] According to the historian Julie Wells, this image of the small stream running red with the blood of the warriors 'has stuck most vividly in the minds of both black and white in generations following the battle'.[6] There is a moving illustration by one of the youthful Xhosa artists of the Egazini Outreach Project in Wells's account of the battle. The text accompanying the picture reads, 'History says that many warriors tried to hide in the river near the battlefield. Here they drowned and the water turned red with their blood. Therefore the bottom half of my picture also shows how the people are drowning.'[7]

According to the missionary Stephen Kay, 'the slaughter was great for so brief a conflict'.[8] The British lost three men killed and five wounded in the battle, but Xhosa casualties were estimated between one and two thousand. Thomas Pringle, writing a decade later, put the toll at fourteen hundred dead on the field of battle itself with many more dying of their wounds, while Charles Stretch, who took part in the conflict as an ensign in the 38th Regiment, wrote of 'two thousand dead on the field of battle and many more perishing of wounds elsewhere'.[9]

* * *

This event in 1819 marked the conclusion of the forty-year-long struggle for the Zuurveld. The attack by Xhosa forces was the first full-scale military assault on a colonial military post on the continent of Africa, and there could easily have been a different outcome. Noël Mostert asserts that 'Grahamstown was the most significant battle of

the nineteenth century in South Africa, for, had Nxele [Makhanda] succeeded, the history and character of frontier South Africa indubitably
would have been quite different from what followed'.[10] What followed
was in fact the settlement of thousands of British settlers, who secured
the frontier area for the British colony and initiated a new mode of
accumulation: settler capitalism.

The battle was distinctive in several ways. Being usually focused
on capturing cattle or contesting political supremacy, precolonial wars
among African chiefdoms in this region tended to be relatively blood-
less. But this battle of 1819 involved many deaths and was about more
than cattle – it was about land, the crucial productive resource upon
which both animals and people depended. Success for Makhanda was
likely both in terms of numbers involved and the skill and courage of
the Xhosa soldiers. Against the British garrison at Grahamstown of
450 soldiers and some armed civilians, including 82 Khoikhoi soldiers
of the Cape Regiment, Makhanda commanded an army of ten thousand. The Xhosa were confident of success, having been promised by
Makhanda the aid of the ancestors and spirits who could turn the settler bullets into water.

Makhanda's optimism must be located in the Xhosa cosmology at
the time. 'The amaXhosa believed that magic affected every human
activity but most particularly war. Every chief had his war doctor ...
The first task was to make the warriors fierce (*ukuhlupeza*) by giving
them medicine derived from fierce animals ... Finally the warriors
were purified by bathing in a river previously prepared with purifying
medicines.'[11] Many Xhosa warriors probably bathed in the waters of
the Kowie River for this reason. Clearly, the Xhosa defeat was due to
the superior military technology of the British forces, but one won-
ders why Makhanda attacked in the daytime when a surprise night-
time raid would certainly have succeeded. Colonel Willshire told
Stretch after the battle that he thought a night attack was planned and
would not have given 'at the time of the fight a feather for [the safety
of] Graham's Town'.[12] The colonist Donald Moodie recorded that the

Xhosa were 'so certain of victory that they had brought their women and children with them, who now waited on the flats behind them with their cooking pots, sleeping mats and food, ready to follow the men into the village after the battle and reoccupy the land which had once been theirs'.[13] According to Stephen Kay, 'had the Kaffirs advanced by night they could not have failed of capturing the place'.

The colonial view was that the attack was the product of Makhanda's foolish pride and paranoia. The most convincing explanation lies, on the other hand, in the distinction between raids and wars. Julie Wells points out that for the Xhosa, as for their European counterparts at the time, raiding and war were two different things, with the latter being highly ritualised around display and the former being smaller events depending on surprise and secrecy. Both sides understood the ritual and psychological value of donning special uniforms, as well as showing and using one's full force and might in a disciplined and orderly fashion. 'While the all-out daylight attack on Grahamstown can only be seen as a failure on the part of the ama-Xhosa, it can be much better understood by viewing it as a carefully orchestrated act of formal warfare. The massive preparation of gathering an army, equipping it with weapons and warriors' attire, not to mention the complex logistics of moving, feeding and sheltering such numbers, all indicate this was a clear shift away from the previously used tactic of guerrilla raiding.'[14]

* * *

A dramatic event linked to the defeat is believed to have taken place at Gompo Rock on the Indian Ocean west of East London. This consists of two rocky headlands separated by a deep channel and surrounded by thundering surf. It is a wild and desolate place, and today access to Gompo Rock is difficult as it is blocked by an upmarket gated housing estate. To some local people it is known as a sacred site where water divinities live beneath the waves. According to the anthropologist

Penny Bernard, it is the abode of 'the People of the Sea'. The story is that in 1814 or 1815 Makhanda called together the thousands of Xhosa here and instructed them to 'dance like springboks' to await a miraculous emergence of the ancestors from the sea. Makhanda claimed that he would be empowered by the ancestors to jump across the channel separating the two rocks. When Julie Wells and I visited the site with local chiefs in 2000, it was obvious from the width of the channel that no person could do so. It also became clear that today's generation of Ndlambe living in the vicinity have no oral tradition of this failed prophecy.

Makhanda was the central figure in the Zuurveld region at this time. The colonial historian Theal wrote: 'Makana was the leading actor in this [resistance] movement. His messengers were everywhere in Kaffirland calling upon all true Xhosas to take part in the strife against the Europeans and the Gaikas [the followers of Chief Nqgika, Ndlambe's great opponent] in thrilling language, promising victory to those who would do their duty, and denouncing the wrath of the spirits against those who would hold back.'[15]

Makhanda's leadership seems to have been based on his own powerful, charismatic personality. As an *inyanga*, a traditional spiritual diviner, he became the closest adviser to Chief Ndlambe, who made him a chief in 1816, giving him jurisdiction over his own territory. He was a complex figure, representing a kind of cultural amalgamation of the predominant beliefs and customs of the area, both Xhosa and Christian. In another sense Makhanda also embodied the human physical diversity of the area, as his father was Xhosa and his mother possibly Khoikhoi. According to Theal, 'His mother was held in repute as a wise woman who was acquainted with mystical uses of plants, and who was skilled in divining events. Her son inherited her ability', to which was added knowledge 'which he acquired from white people with whom he came into contact, especially from [the London Missionary Society agent] Dr Vanderkemp'.[16] Furthermore, he spoke some Dutch and had spent time as a boy among Dutch-speaking farmers. Wells maintains that Makhanda himself 'was the living embodiment of all the complexities and diversities of the eastern frontier melting pot'.[17]

* * *

In March 1819, as the colonial historian George Cory expressed it, 'the whole Colony was called upon to assist in ridding Albany [the area previously known as the Zuurveld] of the pest which was desolating it'.[18] After their victory at the Battle of Grahamstown the British consolidated their conquest of the Xhosa with a full-scale invasion of their territory. The British plan involved expelling all Xhosa from the land between the Fish and the Keiskamma rivers, and creating a buffer zone in the area. The poet and settler Thomas Pringle wrote, 'The villages of the hostile clans were burnt, their cattle carried off, their fields of maize and millet trodden down, and the wretched inhabitants driven into the thickets and there bombarded with grape-shot and Congreve rockets.'[19] The British adopted in all these assaults a scorched earth policy meant to destroy the Xhosa people's economic base.

One of the myths about the Battle of Grahamstown demolished by Julie Wells is that it broke Xhosa resistance to the colonisation of their land. For example, one writer has said, 'The loss at Grahamstown broke the Xhosa spirit ... They were pushed back across the Keiskamma River, starving and homeless. The fifth Cape frontier war was over.'[20] In fact, resistance continued; for example, with an attack on the British military outpost at Upper Kaffir Drift by three or four thousand Xhosa warriors in May 1819. Much of this resistance was based in river valleys where the Xhosa pursued their guerrilla tactics, which involved cattle raiding, attacks on isolated farmhouses, and skirmishes with British forces. After their expulsion, Ndlambe and his followers crossed back westwards over the Keiskamma River until they reached the familiar Fish River bush, and took refuge in the cliffs located about midpoint between the Fish River crossings at Trompeter's Drift and Committees Drift. Wells reports that this is still remembered today by his descendants as the place where Ndlambe hid. 'From this well-secured spot, Ndlambe coordinated with Makhanda and Chungwa, who resided further to the south, occupying the coastal lands between the Fish and Keiskamma Rivers.'[21] But in the end the British prevailed through their use of maximum force.

Three months after the battle of Grahamstown, in August 1819, Makhanda surrendered to the British authorities in a voluntary gesture which, according to Xhosa terms of warfare, indicated his willingness to offer himself as a hostage and begin peace negotiations. While under Willshire's guard in Grahamstown, Sergeant Charles Lennox Stretch reported, 'We could not help feeling for his fallen position and surprised at his lofty demeanour and appearance. He did not speak often, except to request Colonel Willshire, with whom he was acquainted, "not to continue the war on all their cattle". Colonel Brereton had taken 20,000 and his people were starving.'[22] The British first imprisoned him in Grahamstown and then sent him to Robben Island as a prisoner of war, at the same time that Napoleon Bonaparte was being held on St Helena.

Robben Island is a bleak and barren place. For me, travelling there once on the boat named *Makana* was a moving experience. The occasion was the graduation of a group of young people after a course run by Peace Vision, and I had been invited to give a graduation address. I talked a little about Makhanda and requested the students to observe a few moments of meditative silence in the small cell where Mandela had been kept prisoner for seventeen years. Makhanda did not accept his imprisonment with the same forbearance that Mandela later showed. While he was being held, the British started burning all Xhosa huts and kraals in the newly conquered territory and allocating captive Xhosa women and children to farmers as labourers. On the island Makhanda went through a daily ritual of removing his ivory arm bracelet, which was the symbol of his status as a chief, holding it up to the sun at sunrise and sunset, and telling the spirits of his anxiety over the fate of his wives and cattle. He tried to escape from the island but drowned when his boat overturned near the mainland shore at Bloubergstrand. According to Thomas Pringle, 'Several of his companions who escaped relate that Makana clung for some time to a rock and that his deep and sonorous voice was heard loudly cheering on those who were struggling with the billows until he was swept off and engulfed by the raging surf.'[23]

As an early freedom fighter, Makhanda is honoured on Robben Island. Nelson Mandela even suggested that the island's name should be changed to Makhanda's Island. Ex-prisoners often refer to it as Makhanda's University in an acknowledgement of the studies they undertook while imprisoned there. Julie Wells writes, 'Makhanda's reputation as an early model freedom fighter was sealed by the fact that Robben Island could not hold him. In recent times, political activists embraced his name as a symbol of the timelessness of their struggle. What he started in the early 1800s, they completed in the 1990s, they said. Indeed some people feel that the spirit of Makhanda was reborn in Nelson Mandela.'[24] Clearly, Makhanda was, and is, a source of inspiration, a 'torch-bearer' and a 'shining example'.

* * *

Events leading up to the Battle of Grahamstown

The explanation of Makhanda's attack on Grahamstown goes beyond individuals. Three earlier events are critical to understanding his attack: the expulsion of the Xhosa from the Zuurveld in 1811, the Battle of Amalinde in 1818, and the Brereton raid in the same year.

In 1811, the new British governor, Sir John Cradock, instructed Lieutenant-Colonel John Graham to expel all Xhosa living west of the Fish River in the Zuurveld. He urged 'the expediency of destroying the Kaffer kraals, laying waste their gardens and fields and in fact totally removing any object that could hold out to their chiefs an inducement to revisit the regained territory'.[25] Graham assembled a force which included 246 Khoikhoi members of the Cape Regiment dressed in green and 500 British soldiers in their scarlet tunics. For the Xhosa this mobilisation of the colonial armed forces was taken as a signal of war.

On 1 January 1812 Graham launched the assault. 'My intention [he said] is ... to attack the savages in a way which I confidently hope will leave a lasting impression on their memories.'[26] The Xhosa staple crops of sorghum, maize and pumpkin were traditionally sown in spring and began to ripen from mid-December. Graham waited for this ripening. 'We chose the season of the corn being on the ground in order that if the Kaffirs would not keep their promise of going away that we might the more severely punish them for their many crimes by destroying it.' Graham then set about implementing his scorched earth policy, destroying the ripening crops of corn, pumpkins, beans, melons and sorghum, emptying the corn bins, seizing cattle and setting fire to the abandoned kraals. The Xhosa were left destitute and starving.

A British soldier, Robert Hart, at the time a lieutenant in the Cape Regiment, indicated more precisely what was involved in this policy. On 17 January, he recorded, two parties of a hundred men each were sent to 'destroy the gardens and burn the villages. The gardens are very large and numerous; and here also are the best garden pumpkins, and the largest Indian corn I have ever seen: some of the pumpkins are five-and-a-half feet round, and the corn ten feet high.' On the 18th, he said, three hundred men 'went early to destroy gardens and huts, taking with them six hundred oxen to trample down the corn and vegetables in the gardens'.[27] Hart reported that the Xhosa were shot indiscriminately, women (sometimes unintentionally) as well as men, wherever found, and even though they offered no resistance.

Thomas Pringle provided a sympathetic voice: 'Mr Brownlee mentions that the Caffers evinced extreme reluctance to leave a country which they had occupied the greater part of a century, and which they considered as by right their own. The hardship, also of abandoning their crops of maize and millet, which were at the time nearly ripe, and the loss of which would subject them to a whole year of famine was urgently pleaded. But all remonstrance was vain: not a day's delay was allowed them. They were driven out with considerable slaughter, and in a spirit of stern severity.'[28] One of Ndlambe's sons sent an urgent request to the British commander to halt the destruction until the harvest was gathered, after which, he promised, his people would move quietly beyond the Fish River. By way of reply the British confined his messenger in irons and tied him to a wagon wheel with a leather thong around his neck.

Graham spent the next six weeks driving from the Zuurveld those scattered Xhosa groups and chiefdoms that remained. Looking for 'stragglers', the men under Graham's command 'combed the Kariega, the Kowie and the Fish River jungles down to the western bank and mouth of the Fish River'.[29] Having heard that Chief Chungwa, old and ill, had been shot in his sleep by the British, Ndlambe decided to leave and the Xhosa retreated.

On 14 or 15 January 1812, thousands of Xhosa men, women and children made the journey from different parts of the Zuurveld to cross the Fish River. Many of them, including Ndlambe himself, must have crossed the Kowie River en route. Fighting their way through the dense river bush with its mass of euphorbia and milkwood trees draped with creepers, they drove their herds of cattle before them, with their few belongings tied to the horns of their animals. The site where the Xhosa probably crossed the shallow waters of the Fish River has a strong affective force. I was told it used to be marked with a large stone, now covered in the dense bush and reeds which line the riverbanks. As one stands on the hill above the site known as Kaffir Drift where they crossed the river, there is a sense of desolation in the deep silence. It is an unsettling landscape, with distant views of the brown waters of the Fish River winding its way to the sea, its banks lined with giant wild fig trees.

Graham went in pursuit 'as far as the Kowie River but found that the chief was well ahead and had crossed the Fish River about January 15th'.[30] It is said that he was hiding in the rocky cliffs on the east bank of the Keiskamma River. Cradock wrote to Lord Liverpool, the British colonial secretary, on 7 March 1812 saying, 'The whole of the kaffir tribes have been expelled from His Majesty's territories, and

I am very happy to add that in the course of this service there has not been shed more kaffir blood than would seem to be necessary to impress on the minds of these savages a proper degree of terror and respect.'[31]

It was all over for the Xhosa. In just more than two months Colonel Graham had accomplished what so many before him had longed to see done. All government frontier policy from the late 1770s centred on denying the Xhosa claim to the Zuurveld; the aim was to remove all the Xhosa from the area, and expel them to the eastern side of the Fish River. The expulsion of 1812 was the first great 'removal' of the many to come in South African history. 'Some twenty thousand Xhosa had been dispossessed and driven from their homes across the great Fish River.'[32] These were the people Graham had referred to as 'horrible savages, of whom I do not believe there is in God's creation a people more destitute of every good quality'.[33] Graham was ordered to build 27 military posts close to the Fish to prevent the Xhosa from returning and to establish a new military headquarters in the Zuurveld. He chose an abandoned Boer farm set amid a bowl of hills, which became Grahamstown. One reason for choosing this site was access to good water from the springs that are also the source of the Kowie River.

As Stephen Kay wrote, 'this event was productive of the most serious consequences ... There is little doubt that the Kafirs felt very reluctant to leave a country which they had occupied the greater part of a century, a part of which they had at a remote period bought from the original inhabitants, the Gonaquas.'[34] Kay went on to refer to the 'unrighteous conduct of colonists ... towards the defenceless natives'. Travelling through the area by ox-wagon, the missionary John Campbell observed at a site very near the Kowie, 'on the western side of the Bushmans River, a wide valley where the sides of the mountains were covered with Caffre gardens ... from whence they had lately been driven by the military. The skeletons of many of their houses remained and some tobacco was still growing, but the whole of their corn fields were destroyed. Formerly the whole was covered by Caffre villages, but now there is not a living soul but stillness reigns everywhere.'[35] This silence may be felt even today.

The expulsion once led President Thabo Mbeki in 2005 to ask in a parliamentary debate on changing place names, 'Why do we celebrate a butcher?' Mbeki told Parliament, 'Colonel Graham was the most brutal and the most vicious of the British commanders on that frontier. He introduced in the course of those wars, the practice of a scorched-earth policy – that you didn't only fight the soldiers on the other side, but you burnt their fields, killed their cattle, you starved them into submission, you killed them into submission. This place has a name – it's called iRhini, but we celebrate a butcher.'[36]

John Graham was a Scotsman, and his action in the Zuurveld mirrors a similar episode in Scottish history at the same time. During 1819 a total of 1,200 people, almost the entire population of Strathnaver, were evicted by soldiers from their homes. The Zuurveld clearances were carried out in the name of civilisation, the Highland Clearances in the name of agricultural improvement. However, 'It is known that the Clearances were driven by nothing more or less urgent than greed or profit on the part of the landowners'.[37]

Historians like Noël Mostert, Martin Legassick and Jeff Peires have shown that the burning of crops and the destruction of Xhosa subsistence were a feature of all subsequent frontier wars in the Eastern Cape. But this has often been ignored. One writer praised the expulsion as 'a superbly executed campaign, Graham and his redcoats and their Boer and Cape Regiment auxiliaries had turned the tide. They had also restored to the tiny civilized community of South Africa 5,000 square miles of the best watered country in the Cape Colony. Just enough fertile land had been won, with just sufficient defence, for the great advance in law and order, in missionary work and commerce, in education and agriculture, that were soon to be launched from the 1820 settler cities of Grahamstown and Port Elizabeth.'[38]

Distortions of the event continue to appear in surprising places. For example, the expulsion is explained on the Ndlambe municipality

website in these terms: 'War started and when it became evident
that the British guns and horses gave them a huge advantage in the
fighting, Ndlambe moved his people safely across the Fish River.
Outsmarting his British adversaries, he led his people in a night-time
evacuation. They used the horns of their cattle to carry bundles of
household goods. Although the British tried to pursue them, they
could not catch up.'[39] To describe the event as an 'evacuation' is to
obscure the violent nature of the dispossession that took place under
Colonel Graham in 1812.

The second event crucial to understanding the Xhosa attack on
Grahamstown in 1819 was an earlier battle of 1818, which established
Makhanda's power and military leadership. As you drive to Alice past
Debe Nek today, it is easy to be oblivious to one of the great battlefields
of the Xhosa nation. There are no graves, monuments or markers, and
the area is better known for another reason. It is the site of giant earthworms, listed in the *Guinness Book of Records* as the longest in the world.
The earthworms create shallow depressions and mounds of worm fae-
ces over the plain, called *amalinde* in isiXhosa. *Microchaetus* can grow
to more than three metres in length and were once found over large
parts of Africa, but are now restricted to this small region. The haunt-
ing image that is summoned up is of Xhosa warriors trying to hide in
these shallow depressions in the bleak landscape. For here in 1818 was
fought the Battle of Amalinde, between the supporters of Ndlambe and
Ngqika.

The background to this battle was a twenty-year power struggle
between two Xhosa factions, led by Ngqika, paramount chief of the
Rharhabe, and his elderly uncle, Ndlambe. The struggle, it has been
suggested, was not so much a personal rivalry as a conflict between
two different responses to colonisation. As Julie Wells argues, 'rather
than see the relationship between Ngqika and Ndlambe as a fatally
flawed personal power struggle, it should rather be seen as the struggle
of the amaXhosa to define how to respond to the British presence'.[40]
One response, followed by Ngqika, was accommodation; the other,

embodied by Ndlambe, was resistance. Clearly the growing British colonial power had become a mounting problem for all the Xhosa.

In 1818 Ngqika was defeated and three hundred of his followers killed in what Noël Mostert described as 'the greatest and most terrible battle ever fought among the Xhosa themselves. It was without precedent in that it went wholly against the customary nature of their warfare, in which engagements were comparatively soft and casualties limited. The desire to wholly annihilate a foe was alien.'[41] It was after this defeat that Ngqika asked the British for help, which led to the Brereton raid, the third decisive event leading to the Battle of Grahamstown.

In December 1818, on Lord Charles Somerset's instructions, Lt-Colonel Thomas Brereton carried off 23,000 Xhosa cattle in a raid near the Keiskamma River. This provocation, which involved the loss of almost all the Ndlambe cattle, left the people starving and desperate. Thomas Pringle wrote, 'The great majority of the Amakosa tribe had not only been wantonly exasperated by an unprovoked invasion, but were absolutely rendered desperate by thousands of them being deprived of their only means of subsistence. Under such circumstances it would have been very surprising if they had remained quiet.'[42]

This raid was the event that directly triggered the attack on Grahamstown and transformed the prophet Makhanda into a warrior. As Theal observed, 'Makana, who up to that time had exerted himself to cultivate friendly relations with the white man, now spoke of nothing but war.'[43] Between January and April 1819, the Xhosa forces swept over the entire Zuurveld as far west as Algoa Bay, clearing it of the few European farmers it contained. The stage was now set for the decisive Battle of Grahamstown.

* * *

Clearly, Makhanda and Ndlambe were central figures in the history of the Kowie landscape, though when I inquired at the library in Port

Alfred some years ago for information about Ndlambe, I was told that there was nothing.

Ndlambe's life spans a major transition period in South African history. He was born in 1775 in what is now Butterworth. He took over from his father, Rharhabe, and ruled as regent for the young Ngqika at his Great Place (now the site of the University of Fort Hare) from 1782 until 1799, when he moved with large numbers of followers into the Zuurveld. Shrewd and ambitious, by 1809 he was undoubtedly the most powerful chief in the Zuurveld, with thousands of men under his command, and the leader of anti-colonial forces. Like Makhanda, he moved about the Zuurveld area and had cattle stations near the Kowie. The Port Alfred municipality was renamed after Ndlambe because, according to their website, 'Chief Ndlambe, the highest-ranking chief of the amaXhosa, historically inhabited the municipal area'. His Great Place was on the site of the present Enon mission station near the source of the Bushmans River.

Ndlambe has been described as 'the first of several Black South Africans of military genius visible from the end of the eighteenth century on through the nineteenth'.[44] In a 1809 report Colonel Collins wrote of him as 'at the moment, the most powerful of the Kaffir chiefs' and estimated his force at three thousand men.[45] He also described his conversation as 'full of laughter'. The colonial historian Cory referred frequently to his 'considerable ability', 'shrewdness, foresight' and 'restraint'. But while he tried to limit cattle raiding in order to avoid conflict with the colony, he was not always a man of peace. For example, Collins in his report wrote, 'Zlambie [Ndlambe] having taken a fancy ... to the lands near the Bosjesmans River, occupied by some of the kraals of Konga [Chungwa], and the latter having refused to resign them on his demand, his people were driven from them by force.'[46] Ndlambe was initially friendly to the Boers and allied with them against his fellow Xhosa chiefs Tshaka and Langa during the second frontier war of 1793. But he always insisted on the legitimacy of his claim to the Zuurveld. In doing so he was capable of powerful oratory. For example, in 1808, in response to the government's request that he and all his chiefs and their people remove themselves across the Fish River and leave the Zuurveld to the British, he made what has been called 'one of the great cries of South African history'. 'Here is no honey,' he shouted. 'I will eat honey and to procure it I shall cross the rivers Sundays, Coega and Swartkops. This country is mine', and with this he stamped his foot violently on the ground. 'I won it in war and shall maintain it.'[47] On another occasion in 1825, Ndlambe welcomed the missionaries Stephen Kay and William Shaw at his residence (north of Wesleyville) and spoke in words that illustrated his imaginative and poetic powers: 'I have been an earthworm. But today I creep out of the hole. Like wolves and wild dogs, we have been hid in dark places, but today we are called men, and see the light.'[48]

Ninety years old and nearly blind, Ndlambe died soon afterwards on 10 February 1828. Mostert has summed up the momentous changes he witnessed: 'He was the perfect specimen of a powerful chief of the olden times, before intercourse with the colonists. When he was born the whites had scarcely moved much beyond the Cape, although they had already encountered Xhosa on their cattle-bartering journeys to the east ... He had seen more of the early formative history of South Africa than any other man; he died at the very moment that it began to enter the most decisive stage of that evolution. But he took with him the formidable power of the Ndlambe, his people, for he left them no clearly designated heir.'[49]

Following her innovative approach of 'applied history', which allows a popular voice to be heard, Julie Wells has demonstrated the continuities between the past and the present in the widespread appreciation people show of Ndlambe. Her interviews with various present-day amaNdlambe chiefs have established that 'they have very strong, living traditions of their famous ancestor, Ndlambe, as an early freedom fighter, as heroic bearer of the standard of defending African rights at all costs ... Their own sense of themselves is a tradition standing in sharp contrast to what is found in the history books, which portray Ndlambe as an egocentric, power-hungry failure whose influence ended when he died ... They proudly see him as the one chief in South Africa who fought hardest, longest and with the greatest amount of unwavering clarity about the rightness of his cause. As a contemporary Ndlambe councillor to one of the chiefs put it ... to me in a casual conversation "Ndlambe was our Che Guevara".[50]

But while the importance of both Makhanda and Ndlambe as the dominant figures in the Kowie landscape at this time should be acknowledged, the conflict in the Zuurveld was not about personalities. Ultimately it was about access to water and land, a determination on the part of the Xhosa to maintain the land they had lived on for generations against the dynamic of colonial conquest.

* * *

As the river running through the centre of the Zuurveld world, the Kowie was implicated in the struggles described in this chapter. Not only was it a source of water for people, cattle and crops, its banks were the site of violence, its waters a refuge from pursuing enemies and a source of purification for warriors, its pools a means of accessing the ancestors. The Kowie catchment was the scene of many of the early armed encounters between colonists and Xhosa, though much of the later fighting during the final British invasion of 1819 took place in the Fish River valley.

Several rivers are significant in the story told in this book. Not only did rivers mark the boundaries of different Xhosa chiefs' authority, but they were also declared formally by the colonial authorities as the borders of white rule. They wanted boundaries that were clearly defined and unfordable. Yet, as one historian has pointed out, 'The Fish River, which was eventually decreed as the boundary for its entire length, was a most unsatisfactory line of demarcation. For most of the year it was a mere trickle, which presented no difficulties to the crossing of men and animals. Its banks, clothed in dense vegetation, offered ideal cover for marauding parties.'[51] Of course, the 'marauding parties' were the original inhabitants.

The conflict in the Zuurveld was largely about ecological factors, access to land and water, aspects of nature that were invested with powerful social meanings, especially for the Xhosa. Furthermore, the nature of the conflict was largely shaped by these factors: for instance, the country between the Fish and Bushmans was thickly forested along the riverbanks, providing ideal cover, making ambush possible and making it difficult for cavalry to move about. The Xhosa showed great tactical skill in using these forested areas, the hills, rocks, and mountain kloofs, as natural camouflage. The challenges of cliffs and valleys suited the Xhosa's physical fitness, and their knowledge of animal tracks helped them negotiate their way through dense forests. In the forty years of struggle for the Zuurveld, one of the strengths of the Xhosa was this knowledge of the terrain, especially the thick riverine vegetation and the protection it provided. For the British soldiers, sweating in their hot woollen uniforms, it was terrifyingly unfamiliar.

The Battle of Grahamstown in 1819 was a decisive event. When at last the British were victorious in the prolonged struggle to gain control of the Zuurveld, they secured the area by settling five thousand hapless British citizens as a human buffer defended by a line of large stone fortifications. One of them was my great-great-grandfather, who – in the name of 'development' – led a major assault on the river at the centre of the Zuurveld world.

4 | The Harbour

Today it is hard to imagine that for forty years the mouth of the Kowie River was the site of a successful harbour from which small boats sailed as far afield as Mauritius and St Helena, important staging posts on the Cape and Indian trading routes. In 1884 a total of 86 ships entered the harbour, including 30 steamers and 12 sailing ships, and moored at what is now Wharf Street in Port Alfred. But this 'success' was short-lived and involved a massive assault on the river's integrity, a challenge to T.S. Eliot's image of rivers as 'strong brown gods'.[1] According to an environmentalist, the harbour development involved 'a few men's blind pursuit of personal fortune' and 'triggered the steady decline of the Kowie estuary'.[2] One of these men was my great-great-grandfather William Cock, who was among the four thousand British settlers allocated land in the Zuurveld (renamed Albany in 1814) after it had been cleared of the Xhosa. While William Cock is best known for his attempts to develop the harbour, he also played an important role as a supplier to the military establishment, a member of the colonial administration and a pioneer of settler capitalism.

Before human intervention the estuary of the Kowie consisted of a number of channels and sandbanks which were exposed by the retreating tide. The estuary was about 600 metres in width, bounded on each side by steep hills covered with indigenous forest (now known as the East Bank and West Bank). According to a sketch by the first harbour master, the mouth of the river was at the foot of the hill which formed its left bank and was partially closed by two sandbars, which meant extreme variations in the level of the water depending on the changing tides. The main channel ran down the west side, crossed over at the first sandbank and then carried on out to sea by way of the east bank. The main channel of the river in the lower reaches flowed in a straight line past what is now Wharf Street before entering the sea approximately 300 metres east of the present mouth.

The scene inspired in the minds of some of the settlers images of what could become a busy harbour. As in many colonial enterprises, their commitment to 'progress' meant increasing human power over nature, imposing civilisation on unruly wilderness and its 'savage' inhabitants. As Alexis de Tocqueville wrote of North America, most European settlers were 'insensible to the beauty and wonder of the wilderness. Their eyes are fixed on another sight, their own march across these wilds, draining swamps, turning the course of rivers, peopling solitudes and subduing nature.'[3] An exception in the South African case to this 'insensibility' was the poet Thomas Pringle, one of the 1820 settlers. He found that 'the general aspect of the country was … fresh, pleasing and picturesque. The verdant pastures and smooth, grassy knolls formed an agreeable contrast with the dark masses of forest which clothed the broken ground near the river courses.'[4]

The British plan was for the 1820 settlers to constitute a buffer so as to secure and stabilise the Eastern Cape frontier for the colony. The idea of promoting immigration to barricade the eastern border against the Xhosa was first proposed by Colonel Collins after his tour of the area in 1809, and was later taken up by the governor of the Cape, Lord Charles Somerset. He wrote to the colonial secretary, Lord Bathurst, describing the area as 'the most beautiful and fertile part of the settlement. I know not how to give an idea of it, unless by saying that it resembles a succession of Parks from the Bosjeman's to the Great Fish River.'[5]

The other purpose of settlement was to relieve the social tensions in Britain after the Napoleonic Wars and the social dislocation of the

Industrial Revolution. There was not only much unemployment, poverty and hardship in Britain at the time, but also rising levels of protest and civil disobedience. The historian Timothy Keegan portrays the emigration as a strategy of political containment: 'the emigration to South Africa of some 4,000 people in 1819–20 originated as a domestic political gesture, designed to pull the teeth from the forces of radicalism. It was the most ambitious state-aided emigration scheme yet, and nothing on the same scale was to be repeated.'[6]

We should not underestimate the hardships that the 1820 settlers faced on their arrival. Many of the extant settler diaries reflect lives of acute anxiety and deprivation. Some made hats out of wild date-palm leaves, sewed clothes from sheepskins and lived on pumpkin and maize. They experienced locusts, drought and blight on their wheat. Within a short time, many had to leave their allotments in the countryside and search for work in the few towns that had sprung up in the Albany district.

The extent of the fear that suffused settler lives is illustrated by an account from the missionary Stephen Kay, who described how 'a settler party agitated one evening as they thought that the Kaffirs [Xhosa] were coming, because their fires had been discovered on the adjacent hills, between the Kowie and the Kasouga rivers, but the formidable and much-dreaded host turned out to be a swarm of fireflies'.[7] Visiting St John's Church in Bathurst or the farmhouse at Barville Park or the beautiful stone St Mary's Church at Cuylerville in the Shaw Park area, one can but feel sympathy for their struggle to establish their lives in a strange and remote part of the world.

The emigrants from Bailie's party settled in Cuylerville, between Bathurst and the Fish River. This was one of the biggest and wealthiest groups, consisting of skilled tradesmen and professionals, some of whom brought indentured servants with them. But they all experienced considerable hardship living in the dense bush near the little stream called the Torrens (also named the Lushington), a tributary of the Kowie. The building that doubled as school and church also provided shelter for the scattered settlers in the district during both the frontier wars of 1846 and 1850. During the 1846 War of the Axe, 66 people stayed in this little church for more than a year, living fear-filled lives. Water was obtained from the Torrens and supplies of food often ran low. Letitia Harriet Cock wrote, 'During one attack on Cuylerville the natives tried to dislodge the defenders from the kopje overlooking the building and the kraal holding the cattle. This attempt failed, whereupon the natives set fire to the long dry grass after dark, hoping to dislodge the defenders and stampede the cattle.'[8] The present church is the third to be erected on this site, having been burnt down and rebuilt twice, and the morning services held there on the first Sunday of every month still attract a small handful of people, some descended from the original settler party.

There is a tragic pathos to some of the initial encounters between the settlers and the Xhosa. An illustration of the mutual incomprehension, suspicion and injustice at play occurred in 1822 at the Clay Pits, near the Kowie River, where the Xhosa traditionally obtained the red ochre they used for ritual and practical purposes. The 1820 settler Thomas Stubbs wrote, 'We were still living in tents when a group of Xhosa approached calling "morrow, morrow" [molo, molo]. He [the neighbour who had been summoned] brought them to the tents ... My mother motioned them to sit down, and then we saw they were all women with long sticks in their hands. We gave them a lot of settlers' bread, hard biscuit. It was not long before a lot of [settler] men arrived from our neighbours and made all the old women prisoners. They then searched the clay pits and found a lot more. They were all taken to Grahamstown and we were given to understand were hired out to farmers.'[9] Stubbs commented, 'This was the first piece of injustice done to the natives by the Government, and this we had to suffer for afterwards.' Of course, the 'first injustice' was the dispossession of the original inhabitants of the Zuurveld, the Khoikhoi and the Xhosa. But most of the 1820 settlers seem to have been unaware that they had been allocated land long claimed and inhabited by the Xhosa. Instead there was a corroding fear 'of the menace of theft, murder and concerted attacks'.[10]

* * *

Many parties of settlers crossed the Kowie River on the way to their allotted locations after landing at Algoa Bay, the site of what would become Port Elizabeth. The Kowie River was central in the planned allocation of land to them. A letter from the acting governor, Sir Rufane Donkin, to Lord Bathurst of 22 May 1820 stated that the majority of the settlers would be assembled on or near the central and lower parts of the river.

The site where the first party crossed the river was about a half-mile from the sea, and is now marked by a stone plinth. This was re-erected on Settlers' Day in 1956. My mother attended the event as a town councillor and I remember her being much moved by the occasion. It seemed to evoke a sense of reverence for the courage of the immigrants, made up of 500 men, women and children from the parties led by Bailie, Carlisle, Rowles, Owen, Mandy, Scott and Crause, with 96 ox-wagons. The crossing was hazardous because it was impossible to get all the wagons across at low tide and a young boy, Francis Stanley, drowned in the process.

Establishing a harbour at the mouth of the Kowie River was part of the British colonial agenda from very early on. In 1820 a British officer, Lieutenant John Biddulph, visited the Kowie River mouth and investigated the possibility of establishing a port there. With another British soldier, Captain Charles Trappes, he drew a map of the estuary and established that at the river mouth tides rose sufficiently to admit vessels of up to about 120 tons. On 23 October 1820 he sent a sketch of the estuary to the colonial secretary, insisting that 'the success of the settlement much depends upon the navigation of the river'.[11]

On the basis of this information, the acting governor, Sir Rufane Donkin, inspected the Kowie in June 1821. Subsequently he ordered the building of a schooner of light draught to sail between Algoa Bay and the Kowie. He appointed Mr Dyson as harbour master and pilot at £45 per annum with a small house to be built for him, and had erected a flagstaff on the tall hill on the left bank of the river to communicate with ships at sea. This was the core of the tiny establishment at the river mouth which was named Port Kowie in August 1821. After one unsuccessful attempt, the schooner *Elizabeth* became the first ship to enter the Kowie River on 9 November 1821. (The success of the *Elizabeth* was short-lived and she was wrecked at Cape Recife on her third voyage.) At this time the main outlet to the sea was under the eastern hill. Ships would anchor offshore and cargoes were brought in by lighters.

The issues that would become controversial, such as straightening the river and using a dredger to clear the sandbanks, date back to 1823. In that year Captain Joseph Nourse examined the Kowie River and reported to the governor. He had been 16 miles upstream and recorded a depth of 24 feet for some miles. He proposed that the course of the river should be straightened from the sandbar up to the straighter and deeper reaches above the sand beds and suggested the use of a steam dredger (powered by wood from the riverbanks) for deepening and widening the mouth. He suggested that this work could be performed by convicts on their way to Botany Bay in Australia. Landed at Port Kowie, they 'could be hutted and fed at a trifling expense'.[12]

By 1823, when Nourse reported, a little harbour town was coming into existence at the mouth of the Kowie. It consisted of some 30 stone cottages, a harbour master's dwelling and a customs house, which had been erected on the hill that formed the left bank of the river. This has since disappeared under the sand and milkwood trees of the East Beach. In 1825 the settlement was renamed Port Frances in honour of Governor Somerset's daughter-in-law.

Nourse's suggestions were the first of many solutions to the difficulties and hazards to shipping presented by the river and in particular the sandbar at the mouth. But it was only in the late 1830s that the first concerted and substantial attempts were made to deal with the natural problems and at the same time expand and develop the harbour. These efforts – once described as 'going to war with the Indian

Ocean'[13] – were principally the work of one man: William Cock, my great-great-grandfather.

Born in 1793 in Penzance, Cornwall, William Cock led a party of 40 settlers to South Africa in 1820 at the age of 26. He took up a settler allotment at Greenfountain farm, near the Kowie River, in June 1820 and soon began the trading activities which would make him one of the founders of settler capitalism. He described himself as 'a young man capable of great endurance'. He wrote in his journal, 'On my arrival I erected a temporary house, enclosed a large piece of land, but firstly the crops failed. I at once saw that I must look to some other means of providing for my family.' He bought a wagon and 100 oxen and with the help of 'two or three good Hottentot servants' broke in a span. 'In 1823 the Government Establishment for supplying the troops was broken up and tenders were called for supplies. Ours [he was then in partnership with Mr Lee] was accepted, and for years we were the contractors.'

In 1826 he visited Cape Town and, learning of the high price of provisions in the British colony of St Helena, he purchased a 'very smart, fast sailing schooner about 135 tons', a vessel that had been a slaver. 'Then I proceeded to Algoa Bay, took in a cargo of beef, butter and about 200 sheep and 18 oxen. Reaching St Helena, the oxen were sold at 33 pounds each (having cost one pound 10 shillings), the sheep for forty shillings (having cost four shillings and sixpence).' He also went with several shipments of beef to Mauritius, where he found 'Port Louis very gay. I was at a party where 250 ladies sat down to supper.' He subsequently won tenders to supply beef to government troops locally as well as to provision military settlements on Mauritius and St Helena, the latter for a three-year period.[14] Through these activities he made a considerable fortune, much of which he spent on developing the mouth of the Kowie River as a harbour.

Cock is certainly a controversial figure, not least in respect of the Kowie harbour. In a rather dismissive account the local historian Eric Turpin writes, 'Over the years the legend has been created that all the Kowie harbour-works and all the ships, whose home port was

Port Alfred, were the outcome of one man's genius and one man's vast wealth, that man being W. Cock. This is unfounded fiction based on Cock's earliest attempts to make a harbour with sand and bushes, but in later years all the permanent works were carried out with company funds, loans secured by the colonial government and, finally, by the government itself.'[15] Quoting another source, he added: 'The Kowie is a dangerous sluit, deep enough to drown a man, but not big enough for anything else.'

Within the family, however, pride in my great-great-grandfather was an enduring theme in my childhood. He was often spoken of in reverential tones with an emphasis on the title 'Honourable', which came with his membership of the colonial Legislative Council. He was a powerful presence, especially during holidays in Port Alfred, where his large, crenellated home, Richmond House, built in 1840 with a flat roof reinforced to support a cannon, covered most of the indigenous forest of Wesley Hill and dominated the little village before it was demolished in 2006.

He had three surviving sons, William Frederick, Cornelius and Nathaniel, and six daughters. He was described to me as 'a gentle and kindly man' and a devoted husband. In an image of colonial domesticity, I remember being told that his wife, Elizabeth Cock, watered her roses with the water left over from the many baptisms that took place in the house. Talk of pirate attacks on his voyage out to South Africa, hostile cattle raiders, and viewing shipping traffic from the 'crow's nest' at Richmond House, all intrigued me. My source for much of this highly coloured view of the past was a rather forbidding figure, Cock's eldest granddaughter and my great-aunt, Letitia Harriet Cock.

With 90 years separating us, we had an extraordinarily close relationship. She lived with my parents and me in Kimberley until she died in 1951 aged 99 years and 8 months. Three personal qualities are most vivid in my memory: firstly, a strange, musty smell about her person which was not unpleasant but which I associated with her long skirts and dark clothes. Secondly, going for walks with her in the grasslands across the road from our Kimberley home to collect different varieties of grass, which I subsequently dried and pasted into a notebook. I was impressed with her knowledge of their botanical names. Thirdly, I remember fragments of her reminiscences of frontier life. She was born at Hope farm on 5 May 1852 near the Kowie and spent many years with her grandparents at Richmond House.

It was Harriet Cock who, at the age of 8, christened the settlement when its name was changed to 'Port Alfred'. In her memoirs she provided the following, very flat account: 'The Duke of Edinburgh [Queen Victoria's second-eldest son, Prince Alfred] landed at Port Elizabeth on the 6 August, 1860. He was a cadet and it was his birthday and he was to come to Port Frances to change the name to Port Alfred. He came as far as Grahamstown and wanted to shoot an elephant, but Captain Talton and Sir George Grey, the Governor, said he couldn't do both things ... so Captain Talton, Sir George Grey and staff and all the notable people belonging to the Government came to Port Frances as the guests of my grandfather. My grandmother was lying dangerously ill at the time and so she was unable to do the christening. I was the only other female by the name of Cock and so I had to christen Port Alfred. I remember two piles being driven into the river before the work commenced. Someone broke a bottle of champagne and I had to say "Port Alfred". All the guests stayed at the castle [Richmond House] and they had dinner there and slept there that night and next morning at breakfast they sent for me to say goodbye.'[16]

Of her grandfather she wrote that he 'married Elizabeth Mary Toy to whom he was married for 64 years, and had 11 children, 9 of whom survived to adulthood ... He built Richmond House (known as "the Castle") in 1840 and the foundations are 10 feet deep. The woodwork, which was all made of oak, was brought from Cape Town to Port Frances in one of William Cock's own little ships. Before they came to South Africa Cock was on the verge of emigrating to Canada when he was approached by the British Government through Lord Grenfell who was a friend of my grandmother and a member of the British cabinet to "take charge" of a group of 1820 settlers. Later he returned to England and settled at Richmond, near London, but he was one of those men who must be doing something, so it wasn't very difficult for his partners to persuade him to come out again in 1836 with the idea of making the Kowie into a watering place after the style of Brighton. The partners started but when they saw it was going to be a failure backed out and left my grandfather to hold the baby alone.'[17]

Cock has been called 'the lord of the Kowie River' and 'hailed as the man who put Port Alfred on the map'. According to Sir George Cory, he was a man of 'great enterprise and indomitable perseverance'. He has been described as 'Port Alfred's most distinguished son ... a pioneer in the development of South Africa's export business ... one of the earliest to extend the coastal trade and at one time owned 12 vessels ... Though reputed to be stern, he was a man of outstanding character, unshakeable determination, great integrity and a deep-rooted sense of justice. His descendants have it that his philosophy of life was based on Bunyan's *Pilgrim's Progress* and it is said that his wife often read a portion from the book to him in the evenings. He was a deeply religious man who gave not only to his own church, the Wesley Church opposite his home, but also to the Anglicans.'[18] According to Ely Gledhill, few could 'match him in ability and energy or match all he accomplished for the development of the country'. While Gledhill's view of him as an enterprising pioneer is shared by writers such as Guy Butler and Dorothy Rivett-Carnac, others portray him as self-interested or as a war profiteer.

In 1838, Cock's company bought land on the right bank of the Kowie River for £1,500. In the same year he started work on the development of the harbour. After much labour, mainly performed by 300 'Hottentots', a new mouth was cut for the river through the sand hills of the west bank. The main river channel was canalised and diverted to the western side of the estuary. In doing so, the large sandbank which blocked the western channel mouth was cleared and the channel itself straightened. It was directed to the western side by driving five rows of parallel stakes into the riverbed along the line of the bank, each row 8 feet from the other, for more than a mile. The rows were wattled like a basket and the spaces between the rows partitioned into compartments, which were then filled with bush, sand and rubble – hence the description of 'the basketwork harbour'. According to press reports of the time, the outgoing tides scoured out the channel, depositing the sand on the eastern beach and so closing up the former mouth. The new channel meant a navigable stretch of about three-quarters of a mile inland and was opened in February 1841. It has been called 'South Africa's first man-made harbour'.[19] In March a small schooner, the *Africaine*, entered the harbour and tied up at a jetty which had been erected at Mary's Cove (now the site of the Ferryman's Hotel), the first vessel ever to enter the Kowie harbour through the new entrance.

Writing in the *Graham's Town Journal* in early 1841, the editor, Robert Godlonton, declared that 'Practical men, who have been spectators of the war carried on against the sand and surf by our enterprising fellow-colonist, Mr Cock, are of the opinion that victory will declare on his side ... We are informed that the result of straightening the course of the river has been such an increase of water power to act on the sand and surf, as to supersede the necessity for flood gates. We congratulate our fellow-colonist on the success of this enterprise. We cannot anticipate too highly the advantages likely to result from it. We rejoice in the success of the persevering and indomitable energy of a British emigrant.'[20] In 1873 a letter in the same newspaper likened Cock to Ferdinand de Lesseps (of Suez Canal fame).

Cock himself wrote privately, 'if I could have foreseen the trouble, labour and anxiety that awaited me in connection with the opening of the Kowie, in the possession of every comfort and convenience, I would have remained [in Cape Town]'. He described his work at the Kowie as 'a very rash, unwise and injudicious undertaking. No plan had been devised. No engineers consulted and an ordinance was never obtained. The London partners withdrew but I had become deeply interested in the undertaking and felt most unwilling to abandon it. I took over the entire expenditure and proceeded with the work.'[21]

As a result of the harbour development, the Kowie River became the scene of much productive activity. Coastal trade increased between Port Frances and Cape Town and extended even to Mauritius and St Helena. Ships with sugar from Mauritius took back cargoes of oats, bullocks, sheep, butter, beans, casks of beef, oxen, goats, grain, hide, hay and tallow. Fishing boats were active and supplied Grahamstown with fish once a week. Two mills had been built on the river, one by William Holden at the confluence of the Kowie and its tributary the Mansfield in 1830, and a water mill in 1825 on the Bathurst stream, another little tributary of the Kowie River. For ten years it produced blankets and kersey cloth until it was burned down during one of the frontier wars. After reconstruction in 1836 it was used as a grain mill. By 1850 Cock's steam mill at Port Frances was in operation; corn and wheat were ground at competitive prices for the Grahamstown market and for British army contracts. One of William Cock's sons, William Frederick Cock, took over this mill in 1851 and sold meal, bran, seed-oats, steam-milled flour and bread flour.

Throughout the 1840s the harbour was used by small sailing ships entering the river mouth, which had been cut from the sand dunes. They were usually small schooners and cutters, often not exceeding 20 tons, and frequently their cargoes were partially offloaded into small boats before they attempted to enter the river. Later, locally built lighters were used to unload larger vessels anchored out at sea. In 1843 the Grahamstown, Bathurst and Kowie Shipping Company was formed with two iron vessels of about 80 tons each to carry cargo. One of these, the *British Settler*, was later (in 1850) lost with a cargo of wool and all hands.

When steamships came into general use, Cock formed the Albany Steam Navigation Company in 1841 and ordered an iron steamship of 40 horsepower, which arrived in July 1842. It was named the *Sir John St Aubyn*, 'after a Cornish friend of my grandmother's', according to

Harriet Cock, and was both a passenger and a cargo ship, with a capacity of 50 tons of cargo and 16 passengers. In the ladies' cabin were three staterooms with two beds each and a private WC. Around the dining saloon were five staterooms with two beds. The ship first reached Port Frances after a record voyage of three and a half days from Cape Town. Her passengers included William Cock and his eldest granddaughter, Harriet. In January 1843 the *Sir John St Aubyn* made two pleasure trips from Berrington's Cove to the confluence of the Mansfield River and the Kowie, the fare charged being five shillings. But at the end of that month it put out from Port Frances to tow the vessel *Sophia* into port. Between the piers the tow snapped and both vessels were grounded. The elegant *Sir John St Aubyn* lay a total wreck at the river mouth.

An important moment in the history of the river was the formation of the Kowie Harbour Improvement Company. Already in 1849 public proposals for improvements to the Cape Colony's harbours at Port Elizabeth, Mossel Bay and the Kowie had been proposed but no action was taken by the government. Then in 1852 the Kowie Harbour Bill was approved and in January the prospectus of the Kowie Harbour Improvement Company, of which William Cock was a director, was published. Half of the capital of £50,000 was to be a loan guaranteed by the colonial government. Cock complained that 'there was a great want of liberality on the part of the government'. He himself was obliged to take nearly £4,500 in shares. He confided in his journal, 'to detail the trouble, difficulties, scorn and ridicule I was subject to, would exceed my power'. In a letter to his son Cock wrote, 'I am quite sick of politics and shall be glad when I can be free.'[22] Overall, the development of the harbour was a very expensive undertaking and over time much capital was spent on the construction of concrete piers, wharves, machinery, railways and warehouses.

In 1852 a notice in the *Graham's Town Journal* announced that the directors of the Kowie Harbour Improvement Company had obtained the approval of the Cape governor for plans to improve the Kowie harbour, and advertised for engineers to supervise the works. James

Rendell was appointed consulting engineer in 1856. The company then set about constructing the two embankments we have today at the river mouth. Progress was slow. The workforce numbered only 80 men initially, including some Cornish miners for quarrying. 'The idea of the straight channel was abandoned, creating an elbow at Cock's mill. From this arose difficulties with navigation and scour. A spit formed on the east side where grounding was frequent. The paralleling of the banks created the dog's leg. In the long run this change was to prove very expensive, owing to the shipping hazard introduced.'[23] In 1870 the Kowie Harbour Improvement Company was dissolved and the government took full control of the development of the harbour until 1886.

The harbour was at its busiest in the 1870s. In 1873, to one observer, 'the river presents a very bustling and busy appearance'.[24] In 1876, 101 ships entered the harbour and imports totalled over 12,000 tons and exports were worth over £86,000, being principally sheepskins, goatskins, horns, hides, oat-hay, barley, mohair, hooves, bones and ivory, which was obtained in trade with the Xhosa.[25]

From the 1870s local resident William Rose remembered small sailing vessels, 'schooners, brigs and an occasional three-masted barque of not more than 300 tons entering the harbour. Most came from England, taking 2 or 3 months for the voyage but many from Mauritius with sugar and from Cape Town chiefly with flour … They seldom took return cargoes, leaving in ballast, which was obtained from the hill behind the wharf … Most of the vessels could only enter at high water and it was generally necessary to send shallow draft lighters out to the roadstead to lighten them of a portion of their cargoes before they could be brought in to complete their discharge and they would often have to lie out for weeks before they were ready to enter.'[26] 'The number of arrivals in the '70s would probably average from 80 to 100 vessels per annum, bringing some 30,000 tons of cargo of all description, nearly all for Grahamstown … Small quantities of wheat from Peddie and also wool were exported.'[27]

Visiting Port Alfred on 27 November 1878, James Butler wrote, 'The port was busier than I have ever before seen it – 3 vessels, mustering

7 masts were alongside the quay, a great quantity of goods had been discharged and a large number of wagons were loading these goods to take to Grahamstown. Besides all this a number of holiday folks were down from town giving the place quite a lively appearance.'[28] He went on to describe how 'the right bank of the river bordering on the sea [is] entirely of sand … If the town ever becomes of any size it may be very pretty and I should think a healthy and enjoyable place of residence … The river just at its mouth is trained out between piers instead of old covering a large swamp.'[29]

Much had been achieved, especially the construction of two piers at the river mouth, which was a massive undertaking. Following James Rendell's recommendation, the famous harbour engineer Sir John Coode proposed the extension of the west pier. The idea was that by extending the western pier a certain distance beyond the eastern and bending it slightly inwards, the current from the eastward would strengthen the force of scour contained in the tide, and so deepen the bar. The results, however, were disappointing. The bar did not deepen as was expected, although the piers were extended in length with rubble and concrete blocks several times, which involved the use of a ten-ton steam crane and convict labour.

Then, as now, sedimentation was a major problem. Constant sand encroachment occurred from the west, so the challenge was to keep the river mouth deep enough to permit the entry of ships. The building and extension of the piers, and the dredging and raking of the river, were all attempts to keep it free of sand, while allowing the velocity of the tide to flush the mouth. This meant continual dredging and training of the new channel. A dredger capable of lifting 300 tons of sand a day, aptly named *The Perseverance*, was imported from England in 1861. The dredge silt was deposited behind the training banks with wheelbarrows from wooden barges.

Local resident William Rose described watching dredging operations during the 1870s. 'All we had was a small bucket dredger, which kept the river clean down to a depth of 10 to 12 feet at low water. The banks on either side of the river have been made by the spoil brought up from the river. It was brought from the barges into which the buckets had thrown it to the beach by means of wheelbarrows – naturally a very slow process.'[30]

By 1874 the dredger was constantly at work, operating with new boilers, and rails were laid for a train to carry loads of stone quarried from nearby hillsides to extend and strengthen the new embankments. The dredger worked constantly in the harbour until 1890, and between 1870 and that year it is estimated 'to have raised one hundred and seventy-three thousand, three hundred cubic yards of sand and deposited it beyond the training banks for reclamation purposes as well as for clearing the channel'.[31] The technology was crude. For example, in 1869 Cock had used a huge rake, towed astern of a tug, which combed down the bar. In 1875, when the depth of water at the bar had dropped to 7 feet at high water and only 2 feet at low water, the use of a rake was again suggested, and a new and improved rake was brought out from England. Indicative of the desperate nature of the silting problem, in 1869 gunpowder was used 'to blow away the sandbar' in an unsuccessful attempt to open the mouth.

The narrow entrance to the river and the ever-present sandbar made entering and leaving the harbour difficult. Altogether there seem to have been some twenty ships wrecked at the mouth of the river. One was the *Elite*, a two-masted brig of about 250 tons, which came to grief at the entrance to the river on a voyage from Hamburg to South Africa with general cargo in 1870. It was carried by the tide over the bar and onto the shore. The *Chanticleer* was wrecked in 1848 when it struck the west pier. The wreck of the paddle-wheel tug the *Buffalo* in 1889 signalled the end of the harbour development. According to my mother, this disaster was an act of sabotage organised by merchants in Port Elizabeth, who were jealous of the harbour development, though her explanation seems improbable.

While the construction of the operating harbour is generally associated with William Cock, it was largely due to the hard labour of convicts and of local Xhosa and Khoikhoi. Much of this labour involved various forms of coercion. In October 1858 the Xhosa employed at the harbour went on strike for better rations and 200 of them marched on Bathurst to petition the magistrate. After 1859 convicts were the main source of labour in the construction of the harbour.

Convict labour was seen by the Cape government as an answer to the problems of labour shortage in the colony, especially in relation to public works. During the 1840s John Montagu, the Cape colonial secretary, instituted a new system of convict labour which came to be regarded as 'one of the most successful systems of convict control in the nineteenth-century British Empire'.[32]

The meticulous reports of the superintendents of the Cape's convict stations, now held in the Cape Town National Archives, paint a dismal picture of the conditions in which the convicts were held. In 1859 the Port Alfred convict station was established on what is now the site of the Kowie hospital. It was designed to hold 600 men, and in that year 100 convicts arrived, bringing the total labour force employed on the harbour up to 350. Convict labour was employed for all the unskilled work on the harbour works and no machinery was used for stone-breaking or for mixing the concrete blocks for the west pier. It must have been exhausting, back-breaking, slow work. Many were employed on the dredger in removing, with barges and wheelbarrows, the material raised by the scoops.

The prisoners were mainly white men or 'good conduct men of the coloured classes'. In November 1861 a total of 32 Xhosa prisoners were also held there. Most of the convicts were young men, though the ages ranged from 27 to 61. They had mostly been convicted of theft, for which sentences varied from three to seven years; there were occasional convictions for rape, for which an offender in 1860 was sentenced to five years. Most of them had no previous convictions.

In 1861 there were 89 convicts held at the station. In that year an official of the Kowie Harbour Improvement Company wrote to the government appealing for 'a further number of convicts to be employed on the works at the Kowie'. The number grew to 200 but it was claimed that 'no satisfactory progress can be made [on the two piers] on account of the small number of men the Board has at its command'. In response to further requests, convicts were sent from the Grahamstown and Paarde Poort (Uitenhage) convict stations. Towards the end of 1874 there were 130 labourers and 190 convicts at work. The free men received 2s 6d a day in pay.

Living arrangements were harsh, even in the hospital where convicts had to lie on mats on the floor.[33] Prisoners tailored their own clothes from blankets, and the quality of the food supplied, particularly the bread and meat, was poor. A letter from the superintendent in 1861 refers to convicts suspected of feigning illness 'receiving the usual allowance of soup and bread and, in some cases, water in lieu of soup'. On 3 December 1862 the superintendent requested authorisation for the purchase of '4 oz rice, 4 oz raisins, 2 oz sugar, half an oz coffee and curry powder per convict for Christmas day'.

The bland reports to the colonial secretary invariably stated that 'the conduct of the prisoners has been highly satisfactory, no complaints worthy of mention having been received'. But sometime in 1874 the prisons commissioner visited the Kowie and described the jail where some 190 convicts were housed as 'simply one of the things which disgrace the civilised communities of the nineteenth century, and consists only of a few square box-like apartments, in which, without exception, criminals of all classes are of necessity huddled together'.[34] The numbers increased to 400 convicts in 1874 and the station then included a superintendent, chaplain and surgeon.

The men worked under strict supervision. In 1859 the superintendent complained of 'much illness and injuries from work on the harbour mouth'.[35] Punishments for 'breach of regulations' were harsh, ranging from 40 lashes to spare diet and restricted rations, solitary confinement, extra-hard labour, an extended period of imprisonment and being placed in chains. In several cases this was for 'planning to escape'.

Thanks in part to this convict labour, for over forty years Port Alfred was the busiest harbour on the south-east coast. Why then did it fail? The most plausible reason is no doubt the sedimentation of the Kowie. One view attributed this to the weather, particularly the strong south-east gales characteristic of the coast which churned up the sand on the East Beach and drove a sand-loaded current along it, depositing it in the river mouth.

According to several sources, including William Cock (as told to Great-Aunt Harriet), the cause of the silting of the river mouth lay in the failure to carry out the plans for the extension of the piers made by both Rendell and Coode. According to her, 'Some time after my grandfather's death, Sir John Coode and his daughter came to South Africa and visited Port Alfred and while he was here I distinctly remember that he said, "If they had carried out my instructions, all this failure would never have happened." He also said to me, "Your grandfather had no backing – the merchants of Grahamstown preferred to back Port Elizabeth rather than Port Alfred." My grandfather spent 75 thousand pounds on the works of Port Alfred and none of his 12 little ships was insured and one by one they were all lost.'[36]

As Harriet Cock's remarks demonstrate, the Kowie scheme evoked bitter antagonism on both political and economic grounds. It became a political football in the battle between rival interests in Grahamstown and Port Elizabeth. This rivalry centred around trade routes, harbours and later railways. The ambition of Grahamstown to have a port of its own at the mouth of the Kowie 'was a constant source of irritation to Port Elizabeth and fostered ill will between them'.[37] While Cock and others like him 'looked to the construction of a port at the Kowie to arrest the relative economic decline of Grahamstown, Port Elizabeth businessmen were determined that with the completion of the Zuurberg Pass [in 1849], the bulk of the trade from all the interior districts … should be drawn via Algoa Bay'.[38]

Another reason that has been offered for the failure of the harbour was the development of steamships, which eclipsed sailing ships. 'When steamships were developed bigger ships were constructed and these required deeper draft. This was the main reason for the fading of the Kowie Harbour, as both Port Elizabeth and East London were deeper.'[39] According to William Rose, 'Sometimes the port authorities would be too venturesome and the tug would meet with difficulties on attempting to enter, the tow rope would break and the lighters would have to land on the east bank and much of their cargoes were abandoned to the insurance companies. This was the principal cause of the eventual stoppage of all shipping.'[40] By 1890 practically all shipping ceased. The large steamships had driven the small sailing vessels off the seas.

Perhaps the most convincing argument for the failure of the harbour at Port Alfred is made by the historian Jonathan Stead: 'without enormous capital resources it was impossible to make and maintain a harbour at that point on the coast. Even if capital and engineering skill had been available the volume of trade would not have warranted the harbour maintenance.'[41]

The failure of the Kowie harbour scheme brings into question the historical significance of Cock's life. This lies in the prominent part played by Cock and other members of the 1820 settler elite in the development of a new mode of accumulation, settler capitalism, which would spread more widely throughout South Africa. This settler capitalism rested in the first place on the dispossession of the indigenous Khoikhoi and Xhosa inhabitants of the Zuurveld, who were then incorporated into settler society as wage labourers. Their dispossession was driven by settler colonialism, but it was settler capitalism which transformed Xhosa land and labour into commodities. It also involved land speculation, the buying up of conquered land for sheep and cattle farms, trade – initially the frontier trade with the Xhosa – and the establishment of banks and financial institutions to provide the capital for these ventures. This commodification of land as private property represented a fundamental break from precolonial society's understanding of natural resources such as land and water being common property. In all these aspects, William Cock was an exemplar of settler capitalism.

Trade with the Xhosa provided a launching pad for his career. Trading as Messrs Cock and Co. of Grahamstown, William Cock operated a trading store at the mission station Wesleyville, near East London, in 1827. Trading did not seem to contradict the 'civilising mission' of the missionaries and 'five strings of beads were the daily wages of a man'.[42] Cock subsequently extended that trade and established a wholesale merchant business in Grahamstown. His investment in the Kowie harbour development and his acquisition of a fleet of 12 ships enabled him to extend his trading networks to Cape Town and as far afield as Mauritius, St Helena and London. Cock also acquired lucrative contracts to supply the British military establishment at the Cape at a time when the increasing militarisation of the Eastern Cape frontier meant a large market for many different goods and services.

In addition, Cock was involved in creating the financial infrastructure to promote investment, trade and profit. The bank he established in Grahamstown promoted credit and commerce and was extremely successful in speculative terms.[43] Cock, along with the rest of the settler elite, also invested heavily in grazing farms along the Eastern Cape coast, on land from which the Xhosa had been driven. With his sons, he farmed cattle on his extensive landholdings and exported wool and beef from the harbour at Port Alfred. As Robert Godlonton wrote in Cock's obituary for the *Graham's Town Journal*, 'elbowing his way and joining with others [he laid] those commercial foundations on which subsequent generations have built'.[44]

Grahamstown and Cock, along with a small group of merchants, became the centre of settler capitalism. For the settler elite living there, 'territorial acquisition and conquest were directly concerned with speculative profit and capital accumulation'.[45] Cock clearly played a part in the dispossession of the Xhosa and the consolidation of colonial power, particularly as a source of supplies to the British military establishment and as a member of the colonial administration. After Cock's appointment to the Legislative Council in 1847, he became extremely deferential to authority, always taking the governor's side. It seemed to everyone that this was to secure approval for the harbour project at the mouth of the Kowie, in which he showed an 'unfailing perseverance'.[46]

Cock was also a keen advocate of colonial expansion and of the Eastern Cape separatist movement, whose supporters came mainly from the frontier, particularly Grahamstown. 'The impulses were not only the need for security (against what Cory called "barbarous and predatory neighbours") but also the desire of a dynamic group of business leaders for an influence in the formulation of policy which would promote trade and allow them free rein for their vigorous expansionist thrust beyond the colonial borders.[47] Cock was certainly prominent among those 'business leaders'.

Further light on Cock's character is shown in 'the convict incident' of 1849. In 1848 the British government proposed sending a shipload of 300 transported Irish convicts to the Cape. The response was one of immediate dismay and outrage. There was unanimous agreement among the colony's white inhabitants that they should not be landed and an Anti-Convict Association was formed. When the convict ship the *Neptune* arrived in Cape Town, the local residents refused to allow the ship to be provisioned. The *Neptune* was boycotted and anyone who had anything to do with it was ostracised.

One of Cock's vessels, the *British Settler*, an iron-built schooner, was then loading at the Kowie for Mauritius, but Cock had her turn round and sail for Table Bay. The vessel entered the bay with a leg of mutton hanging from the yardarm and, some say, it provisioned the convict ship. For this he was boycotted and, as Cock noted in his diary, 'every conceivable annoyance was resorted to'. The Legislative Council became the butt of popular agitation and in July 1849 it effectively collapsed as local members resigned. Only William Cock refused to resign. 'When he was denied accommodation by all lodging houses in Cape Town, he was given hospitality at Government House, and when no washerwoman could be "found to do the needful", he was lent underclothes by his host.[48] The governor gratefully acknowledged Cock's support.

There are a number of positive accounts of his motives in this action. According to Dorothy Rivett-Carnac, Cock 'flew the leg of mutton to indicate his contempt for the inhumanity of those who, in stopping all service to the *Neptune*, hoped to prevent the Cape becoming a penal settlement'.[49] Ely Gledhill maintained that Cock 'will be remembered for his courage during the Anti-Convict Agitation at the Cape in 1849 ... His humanity could not tolerate the idea of starving the unfortunate convicts and he refused to agree with merchants who would allow no provisions of any kind to be sold to the ship.'[50]

But these accounts ignore how the convict issue was embedded in the growing popular discontent with oligarchic colonial rule. As Stanley Trapido demonstrates, the anti-convict agitation was a peg on which to hang the campaign for representative government in the colony. At this time there was intense debate on the nature of government (whether it should be representative or not), including the limits of citizenship (whether it should be racially exclusive with high property qualifications or not). Cock was part of the 'high franchise party of the English merchants of Cape Town and Grahamstown led by Robert Godlonton, with the decisive support of Sir Harry Smith, the governor'.[51] His motives in the convict episode, it seems, were to ingratiate himself with the colonial authorities, hoping that by showing loyalty he could maintain his lucrative military contracts and official support for his Kowie harbour scheme. In a contemporary satirical magazine, Cock's actions were explained in this way:

Cock in council backs Smith with the weight of his talk
Of Kowie-funds Smith is the giver –
So the Hero shall be the Cock of the walk
And the Senator, Cock of the river.[52]

According to the recollections of Letitia Harriet Cock, however, William Cock was opposed to the landing of the convicts and only supplied provisions (flour and salted meat) to the soldiers stationed at Salt

River to prevent the convicts from landing. She wrote, 'My grandfather said he didn't want criminals landed at the Cape any more than anyone else, but there was a right way of doing things and they should have protested to the British Government.'[53]

Cock does seem to have been motivated largely by self-interest. But behind this is the question of how one interprets motive. As Liz Stanley has pointed out, 'individual lives can never be wholly represented … There are always multiple ways of reading and presenting them, so any biographer's view is socially located and necessarily partial.'[54] It is unlikely that Cock felt any compassion for the Irish convicts starving on the *Neptune*, and he clearly felt none for the indigenous inhabitants of the country, not even when the Cattle Killing of 1856-57 brought the Xhosa to the point of starvation.

* * *

The Kowie landscape was the scene of many violent encounters in the wars of dispossession, and William Cock was directly involved in them as a soldier, as a source of supplies to the British forces and as a member of the colonial administration. Cock formed the Albany Mounted Sharpshooters, of which he became quartermaster, and his sons William Frederick and Cornelius participated in several of the frontier wars. There were many armed encounters in the vicinity of the Kowie River. On 5 May 1846 an engagement took place at Richmond Station, adjoining Cock's home. William Cock recorded in his diary, 'the Kaffirs took from me and my tenants about 600 head of cattle. We gave them battle within 100 yards of my house. There were about 300 kaffirs with guns, we were only 20.'[55] Eleven of the enemy were killed. According to his son Cornelius, 'The Kaffir tactics were admirable. The cattle were divided up into lots of about 20 so that a couple of men could look after a lot. Then one troop of Kaffirs attacked us so as to protect those who were driving cattle, while another lot tried to cut off our retreat.'[56] After the war, the British government annexed seven thousand square miles of Xhosa territory between the Keiskamma and Kei, which became known as the Province of Queen Adelaide, with its capital at King William's Town. According to Tim Keegan, this was simply a 'gigantic land grab'. Cock convened a public meeting in Grahamstown in which a resolution was unanimously passed expressing heartfelt approval of the annexation.

For the British settlers in the Eastern Cape, the subsequent war of 1851–3 represented the triumph of civilisation over barbarism. But 'barbarism' is best described by this incident: 'A mob, which included prominent members of the colonial elite and assisted by a few Mfengu, burned down parts of the black locations in Grahamstown, while a group of "gentlemen" destroyed virtually all of the Theopolis mission station and a large section of the Kat River settlement. Setting fire to the huts and houses, the "Gentlemen" carried with them flags which had been produced by their wives and daughters inside the safety of their homes. The flags had a single word embroidered on them: "Extermination".'[57]

Besides his active involvement in the wars, Cock played an important role in providing supplies to the British military forces. Cock wrote in his journal, 'In December 1834 the Kaffir War broke out and the commission experienced great difficulty in procuring supplies ... I was fortunately in a position to render considerable service to the Government in procuring supplies.' According to Timothy Keegan, 'William Cock, the "army butcher" ... was a "made man"' after the war as a result of his meat contracts.' As Keegan comments, 'War thus was not a calamity but an opportunity for these accumulating men. They acquired a reputation as warmongers, a reputation that was to spread and increase as the years went by.'[58] As the settler Thomas Stubbs wrote, the wealthy Grahamstown merchant class, of which Cock was a leading member, made small fortunes as war profiteers and warmongers. 'In England it was believed that the people on this frontier like a Caffer war better than peace, I must say I believe so too.'[59] Stubbs was not alone in voicing this view. 'Unfortunately few contemporaries were prepared to risk libel suits by mentioning names, but certainly these [war profiteers] included William Cock, James Howse and George Wood, all Methodists and members of the circle around the *Graham's Town Journal*.'[60]

Clearly, Cock participated in and benefited from the imperial commitment to the militarisation of the frontier. For the settler elite, it meant expanded markets, war profits and more land through the dispossession of the indigenous Xhosa people. In that sense he was a 'war profiteer' and at least a tacit supporter of warmongering. But was he also an illicit arms dealer? Keegan maintains: 'The settler merchants of Grahamstown continued throughout the 1840s to be a major source of armaments for the Xhosa ... Profits spoke volumes to these men, and guns and powder fetched incomparable profits after the collapse of the buttons and beads market.'[61] There is no evidence that I could find that Cock was involved in the arms trade. But there is also no evidence that I found of his speaking out against such trade, as men like John Philip and John Fairbairn did. Nor did he ever express any compassion or indignation about the plight of the Xhosa or the atrocities of the military, or make any comments that could indicate a liberal, humanitarian worldview.

* * *

The radical interventions on the Kowie River described in this chapter – the shifting of the river mouth and the canalisation of the river – occurred in a highly militarised moment in our history. William Cock was a principal actor in this story. He is still revered in the Kowie area, especially by the many descendants of the 1820 settlers living there. But he was also part of a self-aggrandising settler elite who promoted the militarisation of the frontier, benefited from it, and wanted a long-term, large-scale military commitment to the frontier as the basis for economic development and accumulation. Revisiting this ancestor has meant acknowledging that my revered great-great-grandfather was a warmonger and a profiteer. This is a far cry from the dominant view of William Cock, which has focused on his major role in the development of a harbour at the mouth of the Kowie River.

Cock was an exemplar of settler capitalism, and the Kowie River was central to his concerns and the cornerstone of his commercial success. The following chapter will extend the theme of dispossession by describing a line of continuity stretching from the harbour to the development of a marina on the river in the 1980s, both of which developments are associated with William Cock.

5 | The Marina

'At the edge of the land lie the watery places – the ocean shore, the salt marsh, the black-bellied pond. And in them and upon them: clams, mussels, fish of all shapes and sizes, snails, turtles, frogs, eels, crabs, worms, all crawling and diving and squirming among the sea weeds and grasses.'[1] The American poet Mary Oliver was writing of a very different shore, but her words also describe 'the edge of the land' at the mouth of the Kowie River as it existed before the marina development. As with much so-called development, the commercial value of the land trumped its ecological value.

Both the nineteenth-century harbour development and the twentieth-century marina are often portrayed as 'one man's vision'. In October 1985 Justin de Wet Steyn began negotiations with the municipality of Port Alfred for his company to acquire land adjacent to the Kowie River to build a marina consisting of 355 plots on five constructed islands placed in a complicated set of canals within a 45-hectare private estate near the mouth of the river. This led to an advertisement in the *Sunday Times*, inviting proposals for the development of 'the most valuable and centrally situated tract of land in the town' as a small boat harbour and marina (see Appendix).[2] Subsequently, after the proposal of the Port Alfred Marina Corporation (PAMCOR) was accepted, the municipality transferred 45 hectares of this 'most valuable land' to the developer in what was later described as a 'joint venture between the municipality and the private sector' or, as a municipal councillor said, a 'swap, a *quid*

99

pro quo'. In return for the land the developer had to pay an 'endowment levy' to the municipality on each marina plot sold, and he also secured a lease on the small boat harbour for 20 years at a nominal R1 a year with the option to renew until 2028. According to a longstanding resident, there was an 'outcry' when these terms were announced.

Clearly this privatisation of a public asset raises a number of questions. Were the municipal councillors and the provincial authorities who approved the privatisation of this public land acting in the best interests of the community? Has the construction of a marina on the river and the small boat harbour contributed to the developmental needs of the community, or has it diverted scarce municipal resources for the benefit of a small elite? What have been the ecological impacts of the development?

Attempting to answer these questions has been difficult. Research has involved many dead ends, relevant documents have mysteriously gone 'missing' from the municipal archives, and an official even claimed that council minutes are not public documents. Many individuals have been extremely helpful and forthcoming in my attempt to write the story of the Kowie River, but I have also experienced difficulties in persuading residents to speak openly and honestly about their views of the marina development. I came to realise that the development is controversial in social, political, economic and ecological terms. Much of this controversy revolves around one man.

The marina is generally attributed to Justin de Wet Steyn's vision. He is a 'local boy' who grew up in Port Alfred and went on to become an extremely successful businessman. He still resides in Port Alfred. According to the journalist Don Pinnock, 'there is about him something of the Lord of the Manor of old, warmly welcoming passers-by in his beautiful home on the marina and working for the good of his villagers'.[3]

In interviews, several residents of Port Alfred connected William Cock's construction of the harbour in the nineteenth century to Steyn's marina. While to some both developments were the result of 'greed and environmental ignorance', to others they represented a similar visionary and entrepreneurial spirit. In an unplanned encounter, the marina developer once expressed to me his admiration for my great-great-grandfather and said: 'William Cock is the father of the marina. We couldn't have done it without him.'[4] In an earlier interview with a journalist, Steyn remarked: 'We completed, one could say, the dream that William Cock started when he changed the course of the Kowie River in 1840. Cock's concept was for shipping. Ours was to take this one step further, and add in accommodation. We merely walked in his footsteps and completed the journey, and in so doing, once again changed the landscape of this historical town, in all instances for the enjoyment and betterment of everyone.'[5]

In 1986 the municipal council appointed a team including engineers, a landscape architect, a town planner and consulting environmental specialists to undertake an Environmental Impact Assessment (EIA) and to monitor the marina project through the construction phase. The team reported, 'There are no absolute factors which would preclude the development of a marina and small boat harbour on the site proposed ... The development will be a successful and positive contribution to the ambience and image of Port Alfred.' It also stated that the development will be 'a prestige, high quality development, privacy and exclusivity will be a key feature and this will tend to exclude public access to the area and its facilities. In practice an existing area of public open space serving an amenity function will be lost and replaced by an exclusive enclave of residential development.'[6] Contrary to those who opposed the transfer of municipal land to the marina developer on the grounds that it was privatising a public asset, this document clearly valorised public exclusion.

This document has been much criticised, and recently one of the environmental specialists involved in the assessment, Professor Roy Lubke, acknowledged that 'the silting up of the canals and river was not foreseen. This in spite of CSIR [Council for Scientific and Industrial Research] engineers making a scale model of the proposed canal system which allegedly "proved" there would be good flushing of the system and a minimal of silt accumulation.' Instead, 'the overall conclusion of the EIA was that the major impacts would be beneficial in that the development would boost the socio-economic environment of Port Alfred'.[7]

In an interview with me, Professor Lubke once again stressed the social benefits of the development and minimised the ecological damage. He said, 'Ecologically we could not see any problem; the area was already disturbed, it was not a pristine environment' and 'the salt marsh destroyed was not particularly rich, compared to the one adjacent further up the river at the Bay of Biscay'.[8] At the time of construction, the manager of the construction company who was in charge of all initial work on the marina told the local newspaper that 'the canals would never silt up as they are a good deal higher than the Kowie River and the speed of the water would be so mild that it could not scar the bottom. Silt only gets pushed into river mouths by pounding waves, not by the gentle movement of water.'[9]

With such a positive environmental report to hand, the municipality sent a request for approval and authority to proceed with the proposed development. On 7 April 1987 the director of local government replied to the town clerk of Port Alfred, saying that 'authority to rezone the site for development was granted subject to inter alia existing and any future guidelines to protect the ecology as laid down by the authorities concerned [the Port Alfred municipality and the Department of Environmental Affairs] were adhered to', including 'long term maintenance'.[10]

In September 1987 a contract in the form of a binding memorandum of agreement (MOA) was signed between PAMCOR and the Port Alfred municipality. PAMCOR received a deed of transfer. The agreement obliged the developer to cover all costs (including the R90,000 cost of the EIA) and to pay 'what is formally known as an endowment levy on each erf to the local authority',[11] based on a sliding scale depending on the sale price of each plot. The memorandum also stated that 'the developers undertake to create a Marina Property Owners Association [subsequently called the Royal Alfred Marina Home Owners' Association, or RAMHOA] on which body will be represented the developers, representatives of council, and representatives elected annually by marina residents. This body will be responsible for managing and maintaining in good, clean order and condition, the canals, the tarred road and bridges, the small craft harbour, the tidal swimming pools etc.'[12]

The development of a small boat harbour adjoining the marina was one of the main conditions of the transfer of this land. The council undertook to lease the harbour and surrounding areas to PAMCOR at a nominal rental until 2028.[13] The MOA also contained a reference to an issue which has become increasingly controversial, the dredging of the river. It stated that it was the intention to donate to RAMHOA 'a suitable suction dredger for the purpose of the purchaser and the Association fulfilling the undertaking to dredge the Kowie River mouth, the canals, the small craft harbour and the Kowie River from the Nico Malan Bridge to its mouth'.[14] While this 'undertaking' has been widely interpreted to mean 'obligation', this has subsequently been denied by RAMHOA and the developer.

The developer has acknowledged that official approval of the project was influenced by his political connections, particularly the support of the National Party MP for Albany, Jan van der Vyver. 'He became my partner and I can confirm his contacts in Cape Town made this marina a reality.'[15] In fact, Van der Vyver was one of the three directors of PAMCOR (along with Steyn and Keith Wilmot), which was registered in 1987. Steyn had the support of influential figures not only nationally but also locally, in the person of Angus Schlemmer, who was employed by the Port Alfred municipality from 1982, was appointed town clerk in 1991, and was subsequently the marina manager until 2016.

An informant who was involved with the initial marketing of the marina properties was certain that 'while no money changed hands, everything had to go through the Provincial authorities and there was nothing illegal or underhand'. However, he also expressed the opinion that 'the marina would never have happened today as environmental regulations are now much stricter'.[16] In a similar vein an informant who is a town planner expressed the view that 'since 2008 the Municipal Asset Transfer Regulations, under the Municipal Finance Management Act, make it much harder for municipalities to dispose of land (whether by sale or lease) than before'.[17] According to an Environmental Impact Assessment specialist, 'our understanding was that the developer got the land for nothing'[18] – on the assumption that the marina was a developmental initiative and not a financial investment. As the marina manager described the arrangement, 'the selling price was not the issue. The issue was the benefits the marina would bring to the town.'[19]

On a historic day in January 1989 the bank of the Kowie River was breached at 7 p.m. to begin construction of the marina. The local newspaper, the *Kowie Announcer*, described the event as 'a historic occasion and a festive one'.[20] But one anxious spectator called out, 'The river is emptying ... the water is all going into the canals.' Later, another breach in the riverbank led directly into what would become the small boat harbour. Many of the people who witnessed the event described a strong sense of celebration. Onlookers cheered and the developer sprayed the entrance with champagne. Most of the hundreds of people watching seem to have had high expectations of the benefits the marina would bring to the little town, especially in the form of jobs and increased rates income. One informant reported that a letter was sent by a local estate agent to all ratepayers assuring them that their rates would be reduced because of the extra income the marina ratepayers would provide. This has not happened.

The marina was constructed with 360 plots, each with water frontage either on the canals or the Kowie estuary. The selling price of the plots ranged from R80,000 to R120,000. Today the marina is a very exclusive development and properties sell for between R4 and R5 million, though there are several for sale at much higher prices, reaching R13 and R14 million. Most of these are holiday homes, so there is a low level of occupancy year round. Several informants emphasised that the marina has involved little job creation, apart from the initial construction. There are 'only a few jobs for maids and gardeners and these are not always well paid', one said. In 2014 a local estate agent sold four marina properties at a total value of R14,750,000. He commented, 'The good news for marina property owners and potential investors is that the average marina property value is rising steadily and is currently the highest it has ever been, despite an unfavourable selling climate over the last few years. This further cements the marina as a great property destination to invest in, with a lifestyle second to none.'[21] For many of the owners, this lifestyle involves expensive boats moored at the private jetties adjoining their properties.

The estuary provides recreational water sports such as skiing, boating and fishing. The marina lies adjacent to the small boat harbour below the Nico Malan Bridge. Now run as a Section 21 company, it provides moorings for some 300 small craft. There are a thousand boats registered with the municipality. The recreational use of the river involves some damage, particularly through the eroding impact of wakes from boats on the riverbanks, even though wake-free zones and the designation of water-skiing zones have been established. In addition, the river has been affected by the building of over a hundred jetties within the first 6 km of the main channel of the estuary. Ten years ago it was observed: 'Almost all residences built in the Marina have jetties fronting their property and additional jetties are constantly added with little regard for their environmental impact. All of these protrude into the estuary channel and marina canals' and obstruct the tidal flow.[22]

The marina is now run by RAMHOA, a body corporate duly constituted in terms of Section 29 of Ordinance 15 of 1985. According to the present RAMHOA constitution (dated 21 December 2009), the objects and powers of the association include 'the option to dredge the Kowie River from the Nico Malan Bridge to its mouth, subject to the majority of the Association members deciding to do so'. As we shall see, the issue of dredging the river is extremely contentious.

In trying to understand the different opinions of the controversial marina development, I came to wonder whether there was a subtle and hidden process of 'social silencing' at work. By social silencing, I mean those diffuse and subterranean practices, independent of any individual's intentions, that deter people from speaking out or standing up in public on matters of public interest. As a result, people are prevented from knowing, in the sense of a deep understanding of events and processes. This creates opportunities for confusion, misunderstanding and misapprehension. It also serves to erode public space, weaken political life, and inhibit individual agency and collective organisation.

The murky current of social silencing operates just below the surface of social life in Port Alfred. It spread and deepened after a local defamation case in 1987 arising from the marina development. As one key informant said, 'the court case scared people'. Two municipal councillors who were also estate agents took the chairman of the Ratepayers' Association of Port Alfred, Frank Taylor, to court for defamation, for having said they had enriched themselves from the marina development. Taylor lost and had to pay costs. Despite several approaches he declined to talk to me and, according to one informant, he 'died a broken man soon afterwards'.[23]

The accusation that the marina development involved the 'improper enrichment' of individuals at the expense of local ratepayers or public funds of Port Alfred was the substance of a letter from a complainant, a member of the public, to the advocate-general in 1988. This official's reply to the complainant and the town clerk of Port Alfred is instructive. He wrote, 'As I understand the problem of the Town Council, it was to find additional income from rateable properties without further burdening the ratepayers of Port Alfred. This was an extremely difficult matter since Port Alfred does not seem to be developing and attracting industry which would increase the rates levied. By the development of the small boat harbour and the sale of the adjacent 45 hectares of land for development as a marina, the Council has achieved the object of increasing the number of ratepayers by some 320 and attracting further business to Port Alfred without the expenditure of one cent of the council's funds … The scheme devised, in my view, is a scheme which has only merit and cannot be criticized … I cannot evaluate the ecological impact of this development on the estuary of the Kowie River. However, the Town Council went to great trouble to obtain a detailed ecological report and development of the project has to take place in terms of the suggestions made in that report. Furthermore, the expense involved in obtaining that report, R90,000, is being paid for by the developer. Your main basis for suggesting that individuals have been improperly enriched at the expense of ratepayers or public funds of Port Alfred, is the fact that, of the 8 members of the Town Council, 5 members are in some way or another involved in property development or involved in agency business in Port Alfred and the fact that these gentlemen have been afforded the opportunity of selling stands at normal commission in the marina development.' The letter goes on to deny that there was any impropriety in this. 'I can see nothing wrong … for these gentlemen to have taken part in a decision concerning the marina, otherwise the working of the Town Council would have been stultified, since had they withdrawn, which I do not deem necessary, there would not have been a quorum remaining.'[24]

Today, fear of speaking out has been amplified by the use of lawsuits known as SLAPP (strategic litigation against public participation) against people speaking out about the environmental impacts of developments. This is being widely used, and a case in the nearby community of Kasouga was cited by informants as a source of intimidation. One said, 'The charges can be entirely spurious with no basis in fact.' Recently an 'undisclosed reward' was posted on Facebook for the identification of the anonymous source of an allegation that raw sewage had been discharged into the Kowie River from a new development. The person offering the reward said she was considering legal action if she could identify the whistle-blower who was spreading rumours, so 'their mouths can be shut'.[25]

At the same time, local civil society organisations, whether the largely white Ratepayers' Association or the black South African National Civic Organisation (SANCO), are weak. The local newspaper does not take a strong stand on such issues, the editor describing himself as 'a neutral observer' and reluctant to 'champion the river'. Only a handful of people signed a letter to the environmental authorities in 2015 applauding them for refusing to authorise the further dredging of the Kowie River and in so doing 'having taken decisions in the interests of the environment and the general population'.

* * *

From talking to local people it became clear to me that the marina was an extremely controversial project from its inception. The vast majority of my informants in Port Alfred supported the marina, the most enthusiastic being those connected to tourism and the property market. A local estate agent asserted: 'I believe the marina is a great asset to the town as it draws tourists, visitors and new residents to invest in the town. The municipality receives the greater part of its rates income from the Royal Alfred Marina, while the local population enjoys many work opportunities in the building of new homes, the maintenance of existing homes, and the management and maintenance of the marina.'[26] According to the developer, 'the real benefits are to be found in the so-called economic multiplier effects',[27] including the contribution to the income of local businesses. One informant claimed that the marina generates at least 25 per cent of the rates of Port Alfred and Port Alfred generates 50 per cent of the rates of the district of Ndlambe, although the municipality was unable to provide me with a breakdown of its rates. The marina manager also claimed that marina residents 'contribute an estimated R9 million to salaries and wages of Port Alfred residents', though it is unclear how this figure was arrived at.[28]

These general sentiments were echoes of a 2005 report on the marina development by an environmental consulting firm, which concluded: 'the positive socio-economic effects are undeniable'.[29] But the question arises whether these benefits have been equally or fairly distributed. As one informant commented: 'The extreme difference in housing and material conditions between the marina and township residents dramatises Port Alfred as a microcosm of the highly racialised inequality which scars contemporary South Africa.'[30] The white inhabitants of the town live on two hills divided by the river and, though the roads are increasingly 'potholed', they receive regular municipal services of water, electricity and refuse removal. In the marina the opulent, mainly holiday homes reflect the excessive levels of wealth and ostentatious living in contemporary South Africa. In stark contrast, the township, named Nemato (Nelson Mandela Township) by residents in 1985, is home to thousands of African people mostly living in poverty and, like the majority of Africans in the Ndlambe district, they lack the resources needed to live fulfilling lives. Theirs is a tragic story of deprivation, involving the denial of decent work, home ownership, access to quality education, health care, adequate nutritious food, and, for some, even that most basic of all requirements for life, water.

While there have been significant infrastructural improvements in the township since 1994, the extent of the poverty is increasing and evident to any observer, particularly in the informal settlement of New Rest, where residents maintain they have experienced years of neglect. An illustration of this is the number of people (some 40 when I last visited) who await the arrival of the municipal refuse trucks at the Port Alfred municipal rubbish dump. One informant commented that 'the municipal rubbish dump serves as a larder for hungry, outcast and truant children'.

An estimated 24 per cent of households in the township depend on social grants. In past years when social grants were paid in cash, people stood in queues for days without seating or shade. On one occasion it resembled a scene out of Brueghel: three blind men were being led by a small child and an old woman was being carried in a wheelbarrow.

Despite progress, residents of Nemato do not own that icon of freedom and independence in South Africa: the land on which they live.

However, township residents are not passive victims of this deprivation. There have been petitions and protest marches, and extraordinary efforts by individuals to meet the immediate social needs in the community. For example, for the past nine years old-age pensioner Beauty Mazana has been providing cooked meals for some fifty children during the school holidays, while Gladys Mbendeni, aged 74 and living on the old-age pension of R1,500 a month, has taken four orphaned children into her tiny home and 'every evening they have a full meal of rice and meat and vegetables' – to mention only two of the Nemato residents I have encountered. Most of these efforts are initiated and maintained by older women like them. They are the shock absorbers of the social crisis. In addition, there are a number of feeding schemes, food garden projects and crèches operating in the township.

This crisis-ridden pattern of life in Nemato is typical of the Eastern Cape generally, where there is a heavy dependence on social grants, inadequate access to food, electricity and housing, and poor service delivery. Throughout Ndlambe, wages are low and unemployment high at the rate of 30.3 per cent in the narrow definition (39 per cent for youth unemployment), and 43.3 per cent in the broad definition (which takes into account discouraged work-seekers), according to the 2011 census. Young men are sometimes described as reluctant to work, but much of the work available is poorly paid. One volunteer worker at the local soup kitchen observed, 'Often men are expected to do heavy manual labour, digging and loading, but by 10 a.m. they give up. They simply don't have the physical strength required because they are malnourished.' With little employment available in the area there is a good deal of movement, with all the social dislocation and family disorganisation that migrant labour involves. It is conservatively estimated that 29.7 per cent of people in the Eastern Cape often go to bed hungry, and 6.6 per cent of people lack adequate access to food.[31] When one looks at the income of households in Ndlambe and the cost of a minimum nutrition basket, it is likely that the levels of hunger are higher, even if one takes into account the number of households that benefit from subsistence agriculture. In March 2016 the Pietermaritzburg Agency for Community Social Action's minimum nutrition basket, to provide for a family with a basic but nutritionally complete monthly diet, came to R2,414 for a family of four: two children and two adults. The food basket works out to about R604 per person each month. When one takes into account other household expenses such as transport, burial insurance, electricity and hygiene items, the minimum nutrition basket is unaffordable for 69.8 per cent of households in Ndlambe.

This is the context in which the social needs of the majority should be the priority in any disposal of municipal assets, as happened with the transfer of 45 hectares of the 'most valuable land' in Port Alfred in 1987 to construct the marina. This development seems to have been largely to the benefit not of the township residents but of the developers and the marina residents. And while some township residents were positive about the potential the marina represented for 'development', especially the possibility of jobs, the expectations of job creation have been disappointed in the long term. Large numbers of African men seeking work at R100 a day used to congregate outside the marina entrance, but recently a job-seeker said they had been told by the marina management that they were no longer allowed to do so.

* * *

The marina has had other economic and ecological consequences, not least in terms of fishing. According to the official marina website, the marina 'makes a great contribution to the ecosystem. It acts as breeding grounds for juvenile fish species, protected habitat for vulnerable species, areas for the production of plant tissue and contributors of detritus and nutrients to the estuary.' But several informants believe that recreational fishing has been badly damaged by the marina, especially because of the noise of the dredging. A long-time resident maintains: 'The fishing used to be legendary, especially grunter and kob often caught in the deep holes where the river bends at Kob Hole, Bells Reach, the Old Mill and the wreck ... But now the river has been fished out ... Pencil bait, white sand mussels and mud prawns were plentiful but now the prawn beds have been pumped clean and ruined.' Moreover, in days past, 'local fishing boats going out to sea brought in catches of up to a thousand pounds of various fish including Kabeljou, Redfish, Geelbek, Red Roman and Musselcracker'. Today the commercial fishing industry has been destroyed as access to the sea has become increasingly difficult. As the Gleneagles scoping report points out, 'The shallow channel now precludes bigger vessels from traversing the waterways at certain stages of the tidal cycle, and the sector of the commercial fishing fleet represented by large deck boats were forced to leave and ply their trade elsewhere. The translocation of the fishing fleet was a significant loss to Port Alfred ... In 1986 the value of the commercial landed catch in Port Alfred was R326,046 with contributions to local business (bait, capital expenditure, fuel and maintenance) being in the region of R1.3 million.'[32]

Other informants were insistent that the marina dredging 'had not damaged the river'. This was claimed in 2013 in a somewhat confusing conversation early one morning on the East Beach with the manager of the marina dredging operations, who said, 'The silting of the river is getting far worse. The dredging is endless. We now have to dredge the opening channel, the entrance to the marina, as well as opposite Kiddies Beach... There are only some small sole who are caught up by the dredger. No other marine creatures. No damage is done to the river at all.'

Some would give more salience to the fate of these 'small sole'. Sole are estuarine fishes and one of the smallest, *Austroglossus pectoralis*, was described by the famous ichthyologist J.L.B. Smith as 'rightly esteemed one of the finest table fishes of the world. At one time very abundant, it is today relatively scarce, but still the most important sole of South Africa. In earlier years the stretch between Port Alfred and Algoa Bay was one of the finest soleing grounds of the world.'[33]

A marine biologist told me that 'all our coastal estuaries have been overfished'. This is very serious because many of our juvenile estuarine fish are totally dependent on estuaries. The destruction of the Kowie estuary has been particularly serious in its effects on local fish. As she told me, 'kob and grunter migrate to sea to spawn and the young fish migrate back into the Kowie estuary, which they use as a nursery area and which is rich in food and with less predators ... but through dredging we are changing species' migratory habits ... Spotted Grunter are very skittish and noise, especially in estuaries, will frighten them away.' She pointed out that 'William Cock's artificial walls destroyed the shallow water refuge of small fish, which meant they became prone to larger fish and predatory birds. However, the marina did more damage because it took away a large area of the shallow water refuge. The marina built walls of packed stone, but none of the estuarine species of fish live like that; they burrow into the sediments. Fishing stocks have declined drastically in recent years, especially shallow water species ... Only about 2 per cent of Dusky Kob are left along the South African coast. The decline rate is very high. Spotted Grunter and White Steenbras are going to be red-listed.'[34]

The marina has had other ecological impacts. The most serious is the destruction of the salt marsh, a type of wetland, at the mouth of the river. Wetlands perform valuable ecological functions and are 'probably the most threatened ecosystem type and the fastest disappearing group of inland waters'.[35] They have been described as the 'jewels of the Eastern Cape'. 'The growth of Port Alfred along the banks of the Kowie estuary, together with the canalisation of the lower reaches of the estuary at the turn of the century, resulted in many salt marsh areas being reclaimed or degraded. More recently, the last major tract of salt marsh in the lower reaches of the estuary was destroyed when the Royal Alfred Marina was developed in the 1980s.'[36] The developed area now covers what was known as Blue Lagoon (a tidal bathing lagoon) and the East Flats (which included a municipal camping ground and a cricket field). 'Prior to the construction of the marina, the wetland and

Blue Lagoon not only served an important ecological function, but also were important recreation and picnic areas. As the name indicates, the lagoon was clean and unpolluted, further adding to its attraction. The marina was unfortunately developed as an exclusive gated village ... a public picnic and recreation area was lost to make way for an exclusive private development ... and a wetland was sacrificed.'[37]

* * *

The other significant ecological issue related to the Kowie concerns dredging to control the silting of both the marina canals and the river itself as well as the disposal of the dredge spoil. Although, as a 1982 report by the University of Stellenbosch stated, 'the Kowie normally carries a low siltload ... partly due to the soil type and good vegetation coverage over most of the catchment area', this changed dramatically after the construction of the marina. According to a scoping study undertaken by Gleneagles Environmental Consulting in 2005, 'ever since the construction of the marina and the breaching of the Kowie estuary banks at two locations to provide access to the marina, the degree of marine sediment build-up in the lower reaches of the estuary (the area between the Nico Malan Bridge and the seaward entrance to the marina) and marina canals has become a major concern. Sedimentation is a common occurrence in Eastern Cape estuaries and indeed has always been a feature in the Kowie system. However, the breaching of the estuary banks and the resultant alteration in tidal flow dynamics is directly responsible for the excessive marine sediment loads now present in the lower reaches of the estuary.'[38]

Another scientific source concurred: 'The construction of the Royal Alfred Marina meant that the tidal flow in the lower reaches [of the estuary] was drastically altered, and the extensive silt deposition within the main channel adjacent to this development since its opening is evidence of the impact it has had.'[39] Today sandbanks are appearing in the river and are visible at the surface, not only at low tide, and beaches are developing on the inner curves. The bar at the river mouth is growing so that the water passing over it is shallower and the entrance is consequently more difficult and dangerous to negotiate.

Several local residents acknowledge the environmental damage done by the marina, but often claim that 'the estuary was already damaged' by the nineteenth-century harbour development, which involved the extensive canalisation of the lower reaches of the estuary. Before the harbour was developed, the lower Kowie estuary consisted of a number of channels and islands that migrated across the floodplain. But in the mid-nineteenth century the estuary was dramatically altered: the main channel was realigned and stone walls and piers were built at the mouth. The outcome was that 'for 150 years the Kowie functioned reasonably well as a harbour for small vessels ... Although silting and sanding up did occur, it was not a major problem that threatened the existence of the estuary. Using aerial photographs from 1967, 1973 and 1995 it was concluded that compared to other South African estuaries there was remarkably little sediment build-up, and this can probably be attributed to the relatively narrow, straight and deep artificial channel geometry and to the piers that helped to keep the inlet open, allowing free tidal inflow and outflow.'[40]

The Gleneagles report refers to the nineteenth-century harbour development as marking a time when 'a few men's blind pursuit of personal fortune triggered the steady decline of the Kowie estuary ... With the construction of the Royal Alfred Marina in 1989, the Kowie once again witnessed an irreversible setback due to environmental ignorance, apathy from the authorities and the pursuit of personal agendas at the expense of the greater community. Subsequently due to the excessive sediment build-up in the lower reaches of the Kowie estuary as a direct result of the breaching of the estuary walls, the legacy left behind by those responsible for the development of the marina is not one that is held in high esteem by the majority of the present day community.'[41]

While the impacts of the marina are all controversial, what is not in dispute is the current silting of the river since the marina's construction.

But how to deal with the sedimentation involves deep differences, and there has been longstanding disagreement on the issues of dredging the river and the marina canals and the disposal of the dredge soil into the dune pocket behind the East Beach. What is new is the scale of the silting problem and the differences of opinion on whether the disposal of the dredge spoil is interfering with the natural formation of the sand dunes adjoining the river mouth.

Many documents illustrate the longstanding controversy and disagreement that has waged between RAMHOA, the local municipality, the provincial and national state in the form of the Department of Economic Development, Environmental Affairs and Tourism (DEDEAT), and various civil society organisations and individuals. The crucial question is whether dredging of the Kowie estuary is necessary to maintain 'estuary health and ecosystem functioning' and, if so, who is financially responsible and where the dredge silt should be disposed of.

Dredging is generally viewed as a disruptive and damaging process. Duncan Hay from the Institute of Natural Resources maintains that the ecological impacts 'are usually considerable, covering large geographical areas and of lasting duration. In many instances research has shown only limited recovery of the benthic [bottom-living] community in areas dredged decades before.'[42] When DEDEAT refused authorisation for dredging the Kowie River in 2015, it was on the grounds that dredging was an unnecessary 'drastic intervention in a natural system'.

According to Dr Aidan Wood's analysis of the municipal archives (which I have not been able to access), the Port Alfred Marina Corporation (PAMCOR) made an application to the town clerk on 27 June 1988 in which 'the need for dredging was clearly stated, with the main motivation being the threat of civil action against PAMCOR for misrepresentation should [marina] property owners not be able to erect jetties'.[43] The developer maintains that the marina home owners' association, RAMHOA, have an 'option' but not an 'obligation' to dredge the river. However, many of my informants maintained that the *obligation* to dredge the river was enshrined in the first constitution of RAMHOA. But at the 1991 AGM of RAMHOA this was changed to 'option', a decision that was challenged by the Port Alfred Ratepayers' Association but confirmed by Advocate Lowe (in a letter dated 25 October 2013) and accepted by the Port Alfred municipal council. One informant maintained that RAMHOA was legally entitled to change 'obligation' to 'option', but another insisted that in doing so, they were violating the 'undertaking' that formed one of the conditions on which the land was acquired. While the distinction between 'option' and 'obligation' may seem semantic, it has in fact substantial implications in terms of responsibility for the costs of dredging, which can be considerable.

In 2013 the municipal spokesman Cecil Mbolekwa declared that the Kowie estuary is within the jurisdiction of the municipality and 'dredging therefore becomes the direct responsibility of the municipality'.[44] In an interview in 2016 the municipal manager of Ndlambe told me that 'the Kowie estuary is a municipal responsibility and we have agreed to pay for the cost of its dredging'.[45] This decision does not bode well for the ratepayers of Port Alfred and means the potential diversion of much needed and scarce municipal resources from meeting the developmental needs of Nemato residents. It is at variance with the final Gleneagles scoping report, which recommended that 'there must be no financial burden on the ratepayers of Port Alfred when it comes to financing the operation. RAMHOA must be held accountable for all costs both for the capital equipment, its maintenance and the ongoing dredging operations.'[46]

While reluctant, it seems, to carry the burden of the costs involved in dredging, RAMHOA is insistent on the need for dredging in the first place. RAMHOA has commissioned a number of different studies over the past ten years regarding environmental authorisation to dredge. The conclusion in the various environmental impact studies – from Gleneagles (March and April 2005) to the documents from Afri-Coast Engineers (2014) and Shepstone and Wylie Attorneys (2015) – has been that dredging of the estuary is necessary. But this is based on dubious reasons which conflate the interests of a minority of marina homeowners with the interests of the entire community. In the process the issue of protecting the health of the Kowie River is not prioritised.

RAMHOA has claimed in documents sent to the environmental authorities that the estuary is already damaged, that dredging of the river has been a continuous process over the last 150 years, dating back to Cock's harbour development, and therefore that there is no need for authorisation from the environmental authorities to continue dredging. The need for dredging to maintain the ecological health of the estuary has not been established. The conditions and technologies involved in dredging in the case of the harbour and in that of the marina are dramatically different. The nineteenth-century dredging, for instance, was restricted to the sandbar at the river mouth. Moreover, dredging is extremely damaging to the river and only serves the interests of a minority of marina residents.

The interests of the Kowie River have not been served by contradictory rulings by the state environmental authorities whose interventions have demonstrated equivocation and confusion. In 2007 authorisation was given for the dredging of both the marina canals and the Kowie estuary. Emergency authorisation was given again in 2012 after damaging floods, but this mandate then expired. After another appeal and an EIA process (undertaken by Afri-Coast Engineers), authorisation was granted in 2014 for dredging only the marina canals, but not the estuary or for the disposal of the dredge spoil on the East Beach, as had been the practice. This decision was reversed the following year, provoking one critic to refer to 'the current shambolic vein of environmental governance'. The dredging activity operated initially in a legal vacuum, which was subsequently marked by considerable confusion, legal uncertainty and contradictory rulings from the environmental authorities. At the centre of the controversy was the question whether current dredging requires authorisation in terms of the EIA regulations, which are derived from the National Environmental Management Act of 1998.

An appeal from RAMHOA and the Ndlambe municipality for the decision refusing authorisation to dredge the river to be overturned was successful in 2015. The success of the appeal was based on the understanding that dredging of the river had been continuous since the nineteenth-century harbour development, and that it pre-dated the EIA regulations. The Eastern Cape MEC for Economic Development, Environmental Affairs and Tourism declared that 'the Applicant is not required to obtain an environmental authorisation for dredging of the estuary, dredging the Marina Canals and disposal of sediment as these activities commenced prior to relevant legislation requiring such, having come into effect'.[47] The decision was obviously based on purely legalistic reasons and without any consideration of the health of the living river. According to an experienced environmentalist, the MEC's decision 'clearly was not based on ecological grounds ... It could be regarded as precedent setting and could be cited in any struggles over any activities in any one of our fragile estuaries. It could mean that dredging all over the country could now proceed without authorisation from the environmental authorities.'[48]

The deputy chairman of RAMHOA described the decision as 'a victory for the town'. The mayor, Councillor Sipho Tandani, commended him and other supporters for being 'the champions' behind the appeal. Tandani said, 'The river is the lifeblood of Port Alfred. It's a tourism drawcard. Everyone with this town's interests at heart was concerned. This is not just about the marina; if the river mouth silts up, it affects the economy of Port Alfred.'[49] But there has never been any suggestion of this happening. The 2005 Gleneagles report specifically stated: 'There is no danger of the marina or main estuary channel becoming completely closed due to sediment build-up. The historical manipulation of the mouth essentially guarantees that the Kowie will always be a permanently open system.' A *Talk of the Town* editorial declared, 'Not everyone will be happy with this outcome, but we hope it will be for the good of the town and not just for the convenience of a few property owners who couldn't lower their jetties into the river. If the

Kowie River became silted to the point of being unnavigable, it would be disastrous.'[50] Again, no suggestion has been made of this outcome ever happening.

This decision was described by several informants as a betrayal of the values enshrined in the National Environmental Management Act and of the responsibility of government to protect a fragile ecosystem and balance private and public interests. One person said, 'It is all about the legalities. No one cares about the environment. The decision implies that EIA activities are useless. This is clearly a governance issue. We need a precedent for good governance in the management of Eastern Cape estuaries.'[51] While dredging of the marina canals is clearly necessary, there is no basis for the assertion that the dredging of the estuary is necessary 'to maintain estuary health and ecosystem functioning' (as made in the RAMHOA appeal). Many informants emphasised that RAMHOA's main concern was protecting the riverfront access of some of its property owners.

* * *

The Kowie River is threatened by other initiatives in the name of 'development'. Many residents interviewed in the course of research for this book spoke of their anxieties about the environmental impact of a number of developments on the banks of the Kowie. One is the Riverview Waterfront Estate, a large upmarket housing development owned by the Royal Alfred Marina developer, Justin de Wet Steyn. It is already said to be impacting on the Kowie River and harming the habitat. 'It was alleged that riverine bush was cleared, protected trees damaged, paraffin leaked into the Kowie River from earth-moving machinery, cycads uprooted and a fence erected which reportedly encroaches on the Kowie River bank, impeding access to the river to animals and humans alike.'[52] The developer denied the allegations.

At the time of writing, the Kowie River is under threat from the construction of another development, Centenary Park, which has been described as an 'affordable, partly high-density waterfront' marina, even though the park is situated on a floodplain. In a letter to one of the developers, the municipal infrastructural development director said that 'extensive environmental studies will have to be undertaken in order to assess any damage and give guidance to the developmental proposals so as to obviate environmental opposition that might arise'.[53] This would suggest that avoiding opposition rather than preventing environmental damage is the priority of the authorities.

A letter to the local newspaper stated that 'the proposed development appears to have a complex canal system with multiple entrances – all of which will impact on the flow of water in the river itself, perhaps also requiring dredging ... It seems that the greed of man knows no bounds, and the profit motivation for the developers and those in positions of authority is the sole reason for the existence of such a proposition.'[54]

In December 2014 the municipal council decided to allow the developer 'in principle' to go ahead with his plans for the area and rescinded an earlier decision of 2006 against development on the grounds that the area lies within a floodplain. In other words, the council rescinded a law of nature. Furthermore, the area is categorised as an area of 'critical biodiversity'. A visit by an official from the Department of Forestry confirmed that the Forestry Act had been violated in the clearing of the area but commented that 'it was difficult to act against another organ of government'. The development proposals were resubmitted to the Ndlambe Council in April 2016 and the developer was given the green light to enable him to raise finance for the EIA report, estimated to cost R10 million.[55]

Whereas the Royal Alfred Marina was sometimes lauded as an exclusive development for a wealthy elite, the discourse around the establishment of the marina at Centenary Park is wrapped in the discourse of social justice as benefiting 'lower income groups'. The impact on the ecological health of the Kowie River is not a consideration. Generally, 'development' is understood in triumphalist terms to involve jobs, create wealth and bring about 'progress'. In all these controversies the health of the Kowie River has been neglected. It is often described as 'our main tourist attraction'. Certainly, tourism is significant in the local economy as the influx of holidaymakers in the peak season amounts to 33,000.[56] But this is an instrumental view of a living river.

The threat of residential development is not the only contemporary problem confronting the Kowie. Further threats come from pollution from the discharge of raw sewage, the use of river water for irrigation, and increasing demands for domestic water as the little town at the mouth of the river grows.

At present the Kowie, along with some 60 per cent of our river eco-systems, is threatened by sewage pollution. Sewage gets into the system through leaking pipes, stormwater drains and poorly treated waste water. 'The majority of waste water treatment works in South Africa are either overloaded, mismanaged, poorly staffed or simply dysfunc-tional. The result is that immediately, outside our urban areas, sewage flows back into already stressed river systems or the equally strained coastal environment.'[57] The problem is worsening. Over the past years there have been many reports of raw sewage spilling into the Kowie River when the sewage farm past Centenary Park could not cope with the volume. Poorly treated sewage water leads to excessive nutrients that cause oxygen depletion, fish deaths and the degradation of the eco-system. It is also a threat to human health.

At the time of writing there are still reports of the municipality dis-charging raw sewage into the river. Such misuse of the river will con-tinue with Port Alfred's new sewage treatment plant. At its inception the project manager stated, 'The plant will be a conventional activated sludge plant, meaning treatment of the sewage will be done by means of biological processes with some chlorine added at the end before the flow is released into the river.'[58] The release of the disinfected liquid sludge in effect turns the river into a rubbish dump.

For a long time, the Kowie was the main source of water for Port Alfred. But the increasing demands from the growing town for a reliable water supply have involved a further set of domesticating interventions on the river. When the town outgrew the municipal Mansfield Dam, which drew from the river, it was decided to build a new dam, named after Sarel Hayward, then the minister of agriculture and water affairs. This was built in 1987 on the Bathurst stream, a small tributary of the Kowie. Water is pumped into the dam intermittently on an outgoing tide from the weir built across the Kowie River just above Ebb and Flow. It is then pumped to a balancing dam, via a pipe which crosses under the river, to the water treatment plant in Nemato township.[59] As an ecologist has pointed out, 'this system reduces the fresh water inflow into the river. It reflects the problem of fresh water depletion in all South Africa's estuaries.'[60] Some of our fish species (for example, all our eels and river mullet) need access to fresh water to survive.

The Sarel Hayward Dam has not solved the town's water problem. At the time of writing, residents regularly experience water short-ages, especially in Nemato, Thornhill Township and New Rest. The area known as Ndlambe East, in which Port Alfred, Bathurst and Kleinemond are the main water consumers, currently uses 6 million litres of water a day and will require a projected 14 million litres a day by 2035. At a poorly attended public meeting to hear presentations from Coastal Environmental Services in 2012 in Port Alfred, the options presented were surface water from rivers, groundwater, desalination or recycling. The short-term solution to the water problem was to source groundwater through deep boreholes drilled at a distant farm and bring the water through an underground pipeline to a desalination plant in Port Alfred. This will yield up to 2.5 megalitres per day. The brine created in the reverse osmosis process will be discharged out to sea on the East Beach in an effluent pipe. The audience was told: 'There will be rapid dilution so this will have a negligible effect on the marine environment but some destruction of the coastal forest.' At the time of writing, Amatola Water is developing this deep-level groundwater project to provide water for the whole of Ndlambe municipality.

Apart from meeting the domestic needs of the growing town, there are also increasing demands on the Kowie River for water for agricultural purposes in the form of weirs and small dams for irrigating crops. The major part of the Kowie River catchment area is made up of privately owned farms growing pineapples, citrus, chicory, lucerne and fodder crops. According to Jim Cambray of the Grahamstown Museum, 'pineapples have destroyed the river more than the marina. Other problems are caused by deforestation which has left no buffer of riverine vegetation, the construction of dams means a rush of silt which clogs up the system, the Orange-Fish tunnel goes through Grahamstown and flushes into the Kowie, so the whole river system is becoming more saline.'[61]

* * *

Many of the current inhabitants of Ndlambe Municipal Area are descendants of the original inhabitants, the Xhosa, who were first dispossessed of their land and livelihoods, and absorbed into the colonial economy as a source of cheap labour. More than a century later this pattern of dispossession and cheap labour has continued. Poverty and the lack of employment opportunities have driven many of the descendants of the original inhabitants of the area to migrate to the cities. Twenty-two years of democracy have brought improvements in the lives of the black majority in South Africa, but many, especially in Nemato and the informal settlement of New Rest, still lack access to the means for a healthy and dignified life in the form of 'decent' work, satisfactory housing, clean water, proper sanitation, access to nutritious food, adequate health care and quality education.

Each of the major assaults on the integrity of the Kowie River – the establishment of the harbour and the marina – is associated with the vision of a single man. Both drove change in the name of 'development', which has had devastating ecological consequences and largely benefited only a wealthy elite. In both these ventures, considerations of private profit and promises of public goods, in the form of increased employment and local revenues, have involved negative environmental impacts, especially because of the destructive effects of dredging. In the case of the marina development, the alienation of land to establish the marina involved the privatisation of a public asset. Furthermore, the fact that Ndlambe municipality has assumed responsibility for the cost of dredging the sedimentation created by the marina development means the developers have also externalised environmental costs. As can be seen, the history of this little river raises questions of both social and environmental justice.

6 | Connecting with Nature and Justice through Rivers

Rivers epitomise the connection between social and environmental justice. Recording the story of the Kowie River involves acknowledging the legacy and continuation of deep injustice: the violent conquest of the indigenous population whose descendants continue to live in poverty and deprivation, on the one hand, and the silting and pollution of a river and the destruction of a wetland, on the other.

'Genocide' and 'ecocide' may seem melodramatic terms to describe these processes. However, the experience of many indigenous people around the world testifies to the strong link between genocide and colonialism. This involves more than the expansion of territory. In the South African case, the burning of crops that were about to be harvested and the destruction of the subsistence base of Xhosa society in the 1811–12 clearance of the Zuurveld do fit into Damian Short's description of 'ecologically induced genocide'.[1] So too would the way in which this scorched earth policy was applied regularly by the British colonisers to defeat Xhosa guerrilla forms of resistance. As Martin Legassick writes, 'The attack on the roots of the Xhosa economy became a feature of all subsequent frontier wars.' It was even suggested on one occasion that destroying crops should involve targeting the people responsible for cultivation – Xhosa women. For example, 'in November 1851 the Colonial Secretary Lord Grey proposed that all Xhosa women should be rounded up and sent to the Cape as prisoners'.[2]

The link between genocide and ecocide, in the sense of 'destroying ecological cycles', is evident in this colonial strategy. Ecocide is also clear in the environmental damage involved in both the harbour and marina initiatives at Port Alfred.

* * *

There are many continuities over the 150 years separating the two major assaults on the integrity of the Kowie River: the harbour and the marina. One feature is the reality of continued injustice in the dispossession of the majority of the population. Running through the Zuurveld, the Kowie River was at the centre of this process. During the hundred years of the frontier wars the Xhosa people were dispossessed of their land and livelihoods, defeated and absorbed into the colonial economy as a source of cheap labour. For a time, the harbour at the mouth of the Kowie River contributed to the maintenance of the military establishment on which colonial power depended. More than a century later this pattern of dispossession and cheap labour continues. Instead of mobilising resources to address urgent social needs, the Port Alfred town council transferred what it had described as 'the most valuable land in the town' to a private developer for what one informant described as 'nothing'. Today scarce municipal resources are being diverted to deal with the problem of increasing sedimentation and the environmental interventions and authorisations necessitated by the marina development. In the name of 'development', over the past 150 years the mouth of the Kowie River has become, in the words of Thomas Stubbs, 'a place where money was to be had'.[3]

The outcome is that today the area is a microcosm of the highly racialised inequality which scars contemporary South Africa. We are the most unequal society in the world, with over half the population living in poverty and with a Gini coefficient of 0.65 in 2014. As Ngũgĩ wa Thiong'o writes, 'splendor is built on squalor'.[4] The wealthiest 10 per cent of our population owns at least 90–5 per cent of all wealth.[5] Such wealth is passed on between generations. The official statistics demonstrate how poverty and unemployment are widespread and municipal services uneven. The overall picture is one of a racialised dispossession of the material goods and services essential to leading a dignified and productive life.

Like myself, many of the inhabitants of the former Zuurveld are descendants of the 1820 settlers. 'Port Alfred is known as the very "seat" of 1820 settler history and you can hardly move at times, as there are so many people who are family-related in some way, from that date in history. Pick a surname and you will trip over more than a dozen kin.'[6] Only one of the descendants I interviewed during the course of research for this book expressed any regret or shame about the historical role of these ancestors. He said, 'I don't feel guilty about taking land away from the Xhosas because we developed the land. The first blacks only came into this area in 1776 ... The 1812 clearance was not such a bad event, but after that all the frontier wars pushed them back and that's where we were wrong. They arrived before us and there was no doubt about possession then.'[7] The comment illustrates the 'disavowal of founding violence and of indigenous people', one of the 'defensive mechanisms' that explain the resilience of settler colonialism.[8]

A notice in the *Graham's Town Journal* about the 1919 celebration of the 1820 settlers stated: 'it is estimated that there are roughly 150,000 descendants male and female of those grand and noble pioneers living today'. The notice announced plans to commemorate these 'heroic men and women' through both an immigration and a scholarship scheme. It was intended to select 'boys who will help to maintain British ideals and traditions, and who are prepared to combat that outstanding evil and menace which is so seriously threatening the whole world today, Bolshevism. As we are threatened by the predominance of the Native over the white it is only by the introduction of fresh blood of the right kind, that we can counteract this.'[9] One person to whom I showed this cutting commented, 'The "outstanding evil and menace" today is not Bolshevism but rampant capitalism.'

Besides vast differences in material living conditions, another theme of continuity with the past is racial separation. Even twenty years after the end of apartheid all informants reported that there is no meaningful racial integration in the little town of Port Alfred. Black and white people live in totally different material worlds that are coloured by different degrees of dependence, dislike and distrust. During apartheid I remember a hooter which used to reverberate through the town at 9 p.m. to enforce a curfew whereby all African people were restricted to the township. Today the residents of the marina have surrounded themselves with an electrified fence and strictly controlled access. Outside the marina, I was told, 'We [white people] all live behind barbed wire with our guard dogs and contracts with security companies.' The politics of fear remains and is taking new forms.

* * *

'Precarity is the condition of our time', as Anna Tsing writes,[10] and our shared vulnerability is most evident in relation to water, especially as almost all the water we use in South Africa comes from rivers. In South Africa water is a shared resource, part of the commons that belong to all of us, according to the 1998 Water Management Act. At the time of writing there is an officially acknowledged water crisis.

There are three main threats to our supply of clean water: pollution, acid mine drainage and climate change. A big contributor to the high pollution levels is poorly treated or raw sewage running into rivers. This is a health risk, but the most at risk are people in informal settlements who use river water for cooking, drinking and bathing. According to Anthony Turton, the lack of planning, skills and 'poorly functioning water treatment plants … are spewing about 4 billion litres of untreated or partly treated sewage into rivers every day'.[11]

In May 2010 the Transvaal Agricultural Union and the National Water Forum (NWF) laid criminal charges against three government ministers, including the minister of water and environmental affairs,

Buyelwa Sonjica, for their failure to protect South Africa's rivers from continuous pollution. They alleged that the ministers had failed to protect the right of access to clean water and adequate food production of millions of South Africans, pointing to two main sources of pollution: the mining houses and municipal sewerage systems. More recently, the Green Drop Monitoring Programme of the Department of Water Affairs reported that only a quarter of the sewage released by our 986 municipal treatment plants into our rivers was properly treated.[12] Because of climate change the world's temperature is set to rise by at least 2° by 2050 and fresh water will become increasingly scarce and polluted as the effects of pathogens and toxins are less diluted. South Africa's annual rainfall is half the world average, and at the time of writing there are widespread water shortages as we experience the worst drought since 1933.

* * *

Most of South Africa's rivers are damaged. This means that what has happened to the Kowie River in recent times is typical of a larger pattern. It is estimated that 80 per cent of South Africa's rivers are threatened, with about 30 per cent in a critical condition. Some of our most important rivers are seriously polluted. For example, the Vaal River feeds 60 per cent of South Africa's economy and almost half of the population, supplies mines and industry on the Mpumalanga Highveld, the bulk of Eskom's coal-fired power stations, the goldfields of the North West and Free State, and Kimberley. Yet a new United Nations Environmental Programme report lists the Vaal River and the Limpopo as hot spots of contamination by acid mine drainage and organic pollutants from sewage and industrial and agricultural waste.[13]

In addition to rivers, all our estuaries are under threat. Alan Whitfield, chief scientist of the South African Institute for Aquatic Biodiversity, has warned of catchment degradation and associated elevated sediment loads carried by rivers into estuaries. 'Linked to catchment mismanagement issues are water quality problems which can take the form of pesticides finding their way into estuaries, or sewage waste causing excessive enrichment and pollution of estuarine waters.'[14] Estuaries, together with their associated wetlands and salt marshes, are fragile ecosystems and need to be protected. One review rated the conservation priority status of the Kowie estuary at 31st of the approximately 250 functional systems in South Africa. The rating was calculated on the basis of weighted size, habitat diversity, biodiversity importance, linkages with other environments (marine and freshwater), and rarity of estuary type with reference to biogeographical zones.[15] 'The threats to the Kowie estuary are typical of those to most urban estuaries in South Africa. They include siltation due to the construction of the marina, domestic pollution, and ineffective and uncoordinated management.'[16]

Threats also include the process of marketisation, which reduces nature to 'natural capital' existing only for human benefit, as in current formulations of the 'green economy'.[17] Many of these threats are justified in the name of 'development' and involve the privatisation of public resources. Both the existing marina and the planned Centenary Park marina involve privatising and excluding land which should be protected and shared as a public asset. Hilary Wainwright uses the phrase 'the tragedy of the private' to highlight the fundamentally inappropriate application of the logic of private business, based on maximising profits, to the management of shared resources, natural and social, and the meeting of social needs. The phrase turns on its head 'the tragedy of the commons', which was an attack on the idea that people can effectively manage common resources together for shared benefit. The tragedy of the private 'arises from the presumption that people act only in their immediate self-interest (rather than taking account of mutual benefit and interdependence). The "potential of the public", by contrast, starts from exactly that awareness of mutual dependence and an ethic of stewardship, mutual care and collaboration that arises from it.'[18]

Such mutual care is also necessary to protect our wetlands. Scientists estimate that more than half of the country's wetlands have been destroyed. Often the pursuit of profit is the immediate cause. For example, in June 2013 Exxaro, one of South Africa's largest coal mining companies, recommenced opencast mining at Weltevreden Pan, a wetland which was an important source of water for agriculture and home to waterbirds, close to Delmas in Mpumalanga. On its website, under a section called 'Sustainability', Exxaro admitted that mining activities would destroy the wetland but went ahead, even though in doing so it (like many other mining companies) was in violation of the National Water Act by mining without a valid water-use licence.

The National Water Act of 1998 defines wetlands as 'land which is transitional between terrestrial and aquatic systems where the water table is usually at or near the surface, or the land is periodically covered with shallow water, and which land in normal circumstances supports or would support vegetation typically adapted to life in saturated soil'. Wetlands perform a number of important functions. For example, David Lindley, from the Wildlife and Environment Society of Southern Africa (WESSA), has pointed out that many so-called natural disasters are exacerbated as a result of people altering natural systems like wetlands, riverbanks and catchments. 'Wetlands act like giant sponges that absorb large amounts of water and release this slowly into river systems over a longer period of time. Similarly, intact riverbanks slow down the surface runoff, allowing water to percolate into the ground water, which will then be released more slowly into the system. Unfortunately poor land use practice over the past decades in South Africa has resulted in more than fifty per cent of our wetlands being destroyed.'[19]

Wetlands are not only valuable as flood-control agents, ameliorating the impact of floods by storing and slowly releasing flood waters to river channels, but 'they are ideal natural filters, trapping sediments, nutrients and even pathogenic (disease-causing) bacteria. They form some of the most productive lands on earth, turning more carbon into living tissue than rainforests do. In this way they perform the vital role of absorbing vast quantities of carbon dioxide, the main "greenhouse" gas.'[20] Economically, wetlands are important 'as they provide humans with food, fish and goods such as reeds, medicinal plants, fibre and fodder for livestock. Wetlands are essential for rural communities as they provide drinking water, land for subsistence cultivation and grazing, plant material for construction of housing and the production of crafts, as well as the maintenance of cultural and spiritual beliefs.'[21] They also provide a habitat for food and shelter for a great variety of plants, animals and birds. Appreciating wetlands – what some local people encountered during the research for this book described as 'swamps' – involves grasping the links between social and environmental issues. Rivers epitomise this link.

* * *

Supporting living rivers involves supporting human needs and rights, as well as local ecologies. As the International Rivers Network states, 'Protecting the Earth's rivers means protecting the cultures, livelihoods and vast array of life that healthy rivers support.'[22]

Mobilisation to protect local rivers is growing globally. In 1997, 14 March was declared the International Day of Action for Rivers, and nine years later nearly a hundred such actions mobilised and inspired people. Across the globe, in places where rivers and communities are affected by destructive river-development schemes, tens of thousands of people from at least 34 countries united. Actions ranged from hunger strikes to sit-ins, from dam-site blockades to urban protest marches, children's events to public seminars, spiritual ceremonies to boat trips down threatened rivers. Most of these were local events.

Similar groups are forming in increasing numbers in South Africa. One of the most successful is the Duzi Umngeni Conservation Trust, which was initiated by a group of volunteers walking the length of the river in sections. Both the Mngeni and its tributary, the Msunduzi, are crucial natural resources for thousands of people living in KwaZulu-Natal, but levels of contamination in these rivers have increased. The organisation focuses on linking restoration to job creation. According to the chair, David Still, 'One of the core elements of the campaign is a River Care Team that focuses on a particular length of river at a time, tackling whatever environmental problems are presented. This could be illegal dumping, invasive alien vegetation, industrial pollution, sewage pollution, illegal sand mining and so on. We have provided many people with work experience and training, boosting their confidence and making them more employable by others.' The long-term vision is to create a river custodianship system where the 'respective landowners in a catchment each take responsibility for their section of the river'. They have also engaged children, enlisting 73 schools in their eco-club programme and involving more than 3,400 learners in river clean-up campaigns. Local community members volunteer as 'Enviro Champs' and monitor and report on sewage leaks, illegal dumping and other environmental problems.[23]

Walking a river deepens one's sense of place. The South African organisation Mayday for Rivers has appealed to everyone to walk their local rivers for a few hours or more at a time. Another way of establishing an intimate knowledge of and concern for local rivers is swimming in them. WESSA supports a 'Rivers for Life' extreme swimming challenge, which involves a small group of athletes attempting over a three-year period to swim a distance of 100–350 km in a major river in each of South Africa's nine provinces. The intention is 'to highlight the deteriorating state of our country's rivers and to stimulate action by the relevant authorities, affected communities and the general public towards saving these vital water resources'.[24]

The Kowie Catchment Campaign, a voluntary branch of the Makana Environmental Forum, based in Grahamstown, has a particular interest in the conservation of the Kowie River and its tributaries. This community environmental initiative 'is about caring for the health of our community and our local Kowie River/iQoyi catchment and streams – dry and flowing'. The group encourages volunteers to care for and learn about the Kowie catchment. Their activities include the removal of alien vegetation, the collection of litter, and the education of citizens about the dangers of pouring poisons into drains and how to conserve water by fixing leaking pipes. The chairman, Jim Cambray, said the Kowie belongs to those involved in the project. 'Freshwater is such an important resource worldwide, and yet it is under threat. We all need to learn to care for this precious resource and the catchments from where it comes.'[25]

There has been only one local environmental organisation in Port Alfred of which I know. During the 1970s the Kowie Trust operated for some years to protect the river. The impetus for its foundation was the threat of the 'development' of Centenary Park on the banks of the river. However, it went on to pressure the council to protect the mud banks so that the prawns taken for bait could recover, to stop the Langdon Hotel from discharging its effluent directly into the river, and so on. No organisation like it exists now, and my own efforts to form an estuary care group and oppose the planned threat of Centenary Park have been unsuccessful.

However, there are local stories which illustrate the connection between social and environmental justice and the unifying potential of collective struggle to protect a river. In April 1990 massive concentrations of mercury were detected in the Umgeweni River in KwaZulu-Natal. Mercury can destroy the central nervous system and cause birth defects. The source of this highly toxic chemical was the world's largest toxic-mercury recycling plant built by a British-based multinational, Thor Chemicals. Not only the river but workers at the plant and the inhabitants of an adjacent informal settlement were affected. Effective protests were launched by Earthlife Africa which involved black peasants, white commercial farmers, trade unionists and environmental activists. For one observer this signalled the emergence of a powerful 'rainbow alliance'.[26]

Today many new alliances are emerging, especially in opposition to the expansion of coal mining. This involves a range of issues such as land dispossession, health impacts through air and water pollution, loss of livelihoods, increasing food insecurity, and inadequate consultation with front-line communities. Access to rivers and clean water sources is at the centre of many of these struggles, which are grounded in the connections between social and environmental injustice. According to WoMin, a particularly painful struggle is that of the Somkhele and Fuleni communities, who have always depended on the Umfolozi River as their main water source. But a coal mine has been pumping water from the river to the mine since at least 2007 and has caused the river to dry up.[27]

WoMin is an eco-feminist organisation supporting women in these communities. All over the world women predominate in struggles for environmental justice. This preponderance is not essentialist; it is not based on any natural affinity that women have with nature. The explanation lies in the gendered division of labour, which allocates caring work to women. A central feature of caring is the production and preparation of food and, in doing this work, women are positioned to promote a new narrative of our relationship to nature.

* * *

Rethinking our relationship to nature involves building on Darwin's insight that we are all connected in an intricate web of life, all part of a single ecological community. This is challenging. As Raymond Williams has pointed out, 'nature' is probably 'the most complex word in the English language'.[28] It is a kind of keyword whose meanings are always unstable and contested. Frequently, nature is understood as something external which can be reduced to a set of competing issues, or as wilderness and wild animals, a place for people to visit or escape to wearing sunblock, mosquito repellent and protective clothing. But there is a consensus emerging that nature is in crisis: we have reached the limit of using nature as a sink for our waste products and simply as a source of raw materials for economic activity. All the same, this consensus still maintains a false binary between 'nature' and 'society'.

Even some of the most passionate commentators on the current ecological crisis perpetuate this dualistic thinking. For instance, Susan George has spoken of a new phenomenon in the history of mankind, which she calls 'geocide'. This is 'the collective action of a single species which is committing geocide against all components of nature, whether microscopic organisms, plants, animals or against itself, *Homo sapiens*, humankind'. But she goes on to say: 'ours is the only species among millions that has been gifted with language, tool-making skills and, above all, consciousness'.[29] This statement illustrates not only flawed thinking in terms of the nature–human binary, but the false notion of human uniqueness, what Freud called 'the human vanity factor'.

Over a century ago Darwin wrote of the mutability of species and posed the question why humankind has to claim to be unique. He wrote, 'Man in his arrogance thinks himself a great work ... Why should we assume that consciousness is a uniquely human quality? It is our arrogance. It is our admiration of ourselves.'[30] All the current animal ethological research indicates that humans are less unique than has been commonly thought. It has demonstrated that animals are conscious agents who act with intelligence, emotion and character. Furthermore, nowhere is the animal capacity for complex social organisation better illustrated than in Anna Rasa's account of Dwarf Mongoose bands or in Cynthia Moss's study of the emotional capacities of elephants.

Many people are estranged from nature and, as Robert Macfarlane writes, this estrangement is 'deeply diminishing. We are, as a species, finding it increasingly hard to imagine that we are part of something which is larger than our own capacity. We have come to accept a heresy of aloofness, a humanist belief in human difference, and we suppress wherever possible ... the reminders that the world is greater than us or that we are contained within it. On almost every front, we have begun a turning away from a felt relationship with the natural world.'[31]

This 'turning away' is not universal, yet many urban residents are alienated even from that quality essential to life: water. As Miriam Darlington points out, 'water and forgetfulness have mingled'.[32] For many of us our water supply comes out of a tap, just as electrical power comes from switches. Sindiswa Nobula from the World Wildlife Fund (WWF–SA) writes, 'Many South Africans turn on a tap and get good quality drinking water and because our needs are met we tend not to think about where the water has come from and the journey it has taken to reach us ... We also forget that this is a country with water scarcity issues. We aim to reconnect people to the real source of our water – nature. By highlighting the role that catchments play in providing water, we envision a society where we all understand where our water comes from and how we can better manage this natural resource.'[33]

Some would claim that we have to provide 'rights' for nature, particularly for rivers. In most legal systems today, rivers have no rights at all. In legal parlance they lack 'standing', or the ability of a party to bring a lawsuit in court based upon their stake in the outcome. In 1972 the legal scholar Christopher D. Stone argued that rivers, trees and other 'objects' of nature do have rights and that these should be protected by granting legal standing to guardians of these voiceless entities of nature, much as the rights of children are protected by legal guardians designated for this purpose.[34] Stone's argument struck a chord with US Supreme Court Justice William O. Douglas. That same year Justice Douglas wrote a dissenting judgment in *Sierra Club* v. *Morton* in which he argued for the conferral of standing upon natural entities so that legitimate legal claims could be made for their preservation. The river, Douglas wrote, 'is the living symbol of all the life it sustains or nourishes – the fish, aquatic insects, water ouzels, otter, deer, elk, bear and all other animals, including man, who are dependent on it or who enjoy it for its sight, its sound or its life. The river as plaintiff speaks for the ecological unit of life that is part of it.'[35]

Recently in India, the Uttarakhand High Court declared the Ganga and Yamuna rivers, which are sacred to millions of Hindus, living entities, bestowing on them the same legal rights as a person. This decision followed after New Zealand's Whanganui River, sacred to the Maori people, was first granted living entity status. According to a framework agreement signed in September 2012 between the Crown and the Whanganui River through the Iwi (the local Maori people), the river will be recognised as a person when it comes to the law, in much the same way as a business company. In one of New Zealand's longest-running court cases, the Iwi won for the river the status of an integrated, living whole, *Te Awa Tupua*, with rights and interests. Two guardians, one appointed by the Iwi and the other by the Crown, will protect those interests.

Drawing from Andean cosmology, an impressive South African, Cormac Cullinan, is at present arguing for a treaty on the 'Rights of Mother Earth'. This approach was given expression in Ecuador, when that country changed its constitution in 2008 to give nature 'the right to exist, persist, maintain and regenerate its vital cycles, structure, functions and its processes'. Bolivia has passed laws enshrining the right of nature 'to not be affected by mega-infrastructure and development projects that affect the balance of ecosystems and the local inhabitant communities'.[36]

In South Africa we have a specific challenge, namely, the 'decolonisation of nature'. This is necessary because colonisation historically involved both dispossession to create national parks and neglect of indigenous knowledge, values and practices in environmental management.[37] Land is the central issue in decolonisation more broadly. It is best understood 'as a struggle primarily inspired by and oriented to the question of land – a struggle not only for land in the material sense, but also deeply informed by what the land as a system of reciprocal relations and obligations can teach us about living our lives in relation to one another and the natural world in nondominating and nonexploitative terms'.[38] Similarly, Aldo Leopold's notion of a 'land ethic' echoes Darwin's emphasis on our ecological interdependence, and resonates with some elements of indigenous cultures, which insist on our 'oneness with nature' and our 'interconnection with nature'.[39]

While hunting in the American south-west early in the twentieth century, Leopold shot a female wolf with a pup. He reached her in time to watch 'a fierce green fire dying in her eyes'. His perspective on nature was utterly changed by this experience and he went on to formulate what he called a 'land ethic'. This involves an expansive notion of an ecological community. He wrote, 'It changes the role of *Homo sapiens* from conqueror of the land community to plain member and citizen of it ... It follows that all ethics rest upon a single premise: that the individual is a member of a community with interdependent parts and the land ethic simply enlarges the boundaries of that community to include soils, waters, plants and animals, or collectively: the land. Something is right when it tends to preserve the integrity, beauty and stability of this biotic community. It is wrong when it tends otherwise.'[40] This is most powerful when it is tied to a sense of place.

A sense of place and of belonging to an ecological community is crucial for the ecologist Barry Lopez, who writes, 'A central task facing modern Western cultures is to redefine human community because by cutting ourselves off from nature, by turning nature into scenery and commodities, we may cut ourselves off from something vital. To repair this damage we can't any longer take what we call "Nature" for an object. We must merge it again with our own nature. We must reintegrate ourselves in specific geographic places, and to do that we need to learn those places at greater depth than any science, eastern or western, can take us.'[41]

Such 'learning' of a place and appreciation of its indigenous inhabitants are captured in a passage by the American writer Annie Proulx. In her paean to place about the piece of land in Wyoming in which she chose to build her home, she writes of this prehistoric Indian world as 'diversely layered'. 'Running through everything these people thought or knew, like the vast root systems of grasses that extend deep beneath the surface, as intricate as the lace work of billions of spiderwebs, were spiritual filaments that guided behaviour and nourished rich mythologies. We today can barely comprehend the interconnectedness of their observations of the natural world, their ideas and lives.'[42] Much environmental activism builds on this kind of attachment to place, and draws strength from different forms of rootedness and belonging. Such emotional attachment is a supplement to the large and highly abstract notions of 'the Sixth Great Extinction' or 'the Anthropocene', which do not capture the pain and immediacy of environmental destruction.

* * *

Are rivers 'strong brown gods'? T.S. Eliot's image reminds us that 'many seem to have forgotten the vital and contradictory roles that our rivers play as cleansers and renewers, destroyers and creators, sculptors of landscapes, life-givers and life-takers'.[43] All over the world rivers have endured (but not always survived) being dammed, domesticated, polluted, diverted, filled up, mapped and built over. Don Pinnock writes, 'We've plugged the Tugela, the Orange, the Limpopo and the mighty Zambezi. There are dams on the Congo, the Niger and the Nile. The Mississippi has been halted, the Colorado no longer reaches the sea, the Ganges has been tamed and the Yangtze is a toothless dragon. Every major river in Europe is not only stoppered like a bathtub but turned on and off like a tap.'[44] The Kowie is a little river. Does it have the capacity to withstand the attempts at domestication which this book has described?

Some time ago a scientist warned, 'Activities that have resulted in the manipulation of the Kowie estuary and the steady degradation of what was once a thriving system have come home to haunt those responsible ... The Kowie estuary has reached its carrying capacity and the pressures being placed on its resources need to be curtailed ... [There should be] a moratorium on any further developments ... The estuary will not be able to cope with the additional pressures ... The focus should be on sustainable development, and it is clear that additional projects on a similar scale to the marina and in close proximity to the Kowie estuary that will place undue burden on the Kowie and her living resources will not be sustainable. There are riches offered by the Kowie estuary that go beyond those measured in hard currency. Our natural heritage is priceless and should be preserved for all South Africans, both now and in the future, instead of being sacrificed through greed and environmental ignorance for the dubious benefit of an elite few.'[45]

The 'elite few' included my great-great-grandfather William Cock, an exemplar of settler capitalism who was implicated in the two assaults on the river described in this book. The nineteenth-century attempt to create a working harbour involved the closure of the river mouth and canalisation which, according to Justin Steyn, made the second assault on the river, the marina, possible. Hence he described Cock as 'the father of the marina' established at the river mouth 150 years later. Both 'developments' have damaged a wild, tidal river and raise questions of environmental justice. Both developments also raise questions of social justice about the role of the river in the process of racialised dispossession. This occurred historically through the support the harbour provided for the British military establishment. It continues in the privatisation of a public asset and the diversion of scarce resources to deal with the dredging of the river. What has been termed 'the structural violence of settler colonialism'[46] was replaced by the structural violence of apartheid and neoliberalism.

But this scenario is not inevitable. There are hopeful signs of struggles, grounded in the recognition of the linkages between social and environmental injustice, emerging in contemporary South Africa. The environmental movement is still fragmented, a fragmentation which revolves around a fault line that divides the movement into two main streams: a narrow conservation movement focused on the protection of wild places, plants and animals, and the environmental justice movement, which is organising around concrete issues in the everyday experience of poor people, especially their exposure to toxic pollution and lack of access to critical resources. However, the gap may be closing somewhat. Increasing numbers of people are angered by inequality and the unequal distribution of access to resources, as well as the pollution of the air and water and the loss of wilderness and wild creatures. Perhaps we could learn from the Japanese *Satoyama* volunteers whose work to restore damaged landscapes is also intended to recover a lost sociability and 'remake the human spirit'.[47]

Telling this story of damage and dispossession is not wholly a narrative of loss. But certainly it is coloured by nostalgia. This term was derived by a seventeenth-century physician from the Greek words *nostos*, meaning 'return', and *algos*, meaning 'suffering'. For this physician such 'homesickness' was a serious illness. It involved 'continued sadness, ... disturbed sleep either wakeful or continuous, decrease of strength, hunger, thirst, senses diminished ... also stupidity of the mind', and so on.[48] I think nostalgia for the Kowie River has meant for me an aching kind of longing, a restlessness to return.

Certainly the river has been important all my life. According to Barry Lopez, 'To know a physical place you must become intimate with it. You must open yourself to its textures, its colours in varying day and night lights, its sonic dimensions. You must in some way become vulnerable to it.[49] So writing this book has involved a personal journey during which I have learnt a great deal. This learning also involves a new understanding of myself and the meaning of an identity shaped by generations of enduring, racialised privilege. Owning privilege is clearly a necessary part of challenging the persistence of apartheid inequalities in the present. But we also have to overcome what the ecologist Vandana Shiva terms an 'eco-apartheid'. She describes this as 'a much wider and deeper apartheid [than the South African case], an eco-apartheid based on the illusion of separateness, of humans from nature, in our minds and lives. This is an illusion because we are part of nature and earth, not apart from it.'[50] It is an illusion which is deeply embedded in modernist, dualistic thinking about 'nature' and 'society' as separate entities, instead of as a relational whole. This is a way of thinking which obscures how we are part of nature in the food we eat, the water we drink, and the air we breathe.

A widespread recognition of ourselves as part of nature in an inter-connected ecological community is far off, but perhaps we can connect with our very different histories through our ancestors, and with nature and justice through rivers. Unlike other bodies of water such as dams or oceans, rivers have a destination and we can learn from the strength and certainty with which they travel. This learning could be valuable because the ravages of the past continue in the present, and acknowledging that past, and the inter-generational, racialised privileges, damages and denials it established and perpetuates, is essential for any shared future.

Appendix

Advertisement in the *Sunday Times*,
11 January 1987

Port Alfred Municipality Development Proposals. Small Boat Harbour: Related Developments

The Port Alfred Municipality has set aside the most valuable, centrally situated tract of land in the town for the development of a small boat harbour and related residential development which could, undoubtedly, include a marina.

The land, which is approximately 44 ha in extent, is low lying and consists of a series of isolated lagoons adjacent to the Kowie River.

An Environmental Impact Assessment has been undertaken on the Kowie River and the effect the envisaged and other related development might have on the ecology of the river and adjacent flats area.

The preliminary design of the small boat harbour has, in addition to the above, been completed.

Further information related to the proposal development is available from the Town Clerk, P.O. Box 13, Port Alfred, which includes copies of the EIA and the preliminary design proposals for the small boat harbour, on a receipt of a deposit of R1,000 made payable to the Port Alfred Municipality.

[After the submission of proposals] Acceptance of the proposal by the Port Alfred Municipality is conditional upon the Director of Local Government approving the alienation/rezoning of the land.

The Council's final decision will be based upon the ultimate benefit of the development to the citizens of Port Alfred.

Development proposals will be opened at 12.15 p.m. on Wednesday 11th March 1987 at the office of the Town Clerk, Port Alfred.

Signed H.K. Chapman (Town Clerk)

Chapter 1

1 Joseph Conrad, *The Heart of Darkness and Other Stories* (London: Wordsworth Classics, 1995), 47.

2 Hazel Crampton, Jeff Peires and Carl Vernon, eds, Introduction to *Into the Hitherto Unknown: Ensign Beutler's Expedition to the Eastern Cape, 1752* (Cape Town: Van Riebeeck Society, 2013), xviii.

3 Robert Ross, *The Borders of Race in Colonial South Africa: The Kat River Settlement 1820–1850* (Cambridge: Cambridge University Press, 2014), 19.

4 This was pointed out to me by Tony Dold.

5 Clare Anderson, *Subaltern Lives: Biographies of Colonialism in the Indian Ocean World 1790–1920* (Cambridge: Cambridge University Press, 2012), 22.

6 August Beutler, quoted in *Into the Hitherto Unknown: Ensign Beutler's Expedition to the Eastern Cape, 1752* (Cape Town: Van Riebeeck Society, 2013), 81.

7 Beutler, *Into the Hitherto Unknown*, 119.

8 Jeff Peires, *The House of Phalo: A History of the Xhosa People in the Days of Their Independence* (Johannesburg: Ravan Press, 1981), 148.

9 Aubrey Matshiqi, 'Denial of Unpalatable Truth Is a Road to Nowhere', *Business Day*, 14 June 2016.

10 Amy Novesky, *Cloth Lullaby: The Woven Life of Louise Bourgeois* (New York: Abrams Books for Young Readers, 2016), 3.

11 Rebecca Solnit, *The Faraway Nearby* (London: Granta, 2014), 30.

12 Czesław Miłosz, 'I Sleep a Lot', in *Collected Poems* (New York: Ecco Publishing, 1990).

13 Cited by Christine Hardyment, 'The Strippling Thames', *Oxford Today* 24, 3 (2012), 42.

14 Jeremy Seal, *Meander East to West, Indirectly, along a Turkish River* (New York: Bloomsbury, 2012).

15 Phil Harwood, *Canoeing the Congo* (London: Troubador Publishers, 2012).

16 Olivia Laing, *To the River: A Journey beneath the Surface* (London: Canongate, 2011), 9.

17 Robert Macfarlane, *The Wild Places* (London: Granta, 2009), 122.

18 Laing, *To the River*, 18.

19 Robert Twigger, *Red Nile* (London: Phoenix, 2014), 11.

20 David Harvey, *The Enigma of Capital* (New York: Oxford University Press, 2010), 74.

21 David McCarthy, *The Moth Snowstorm: Nature and Joy* (London: John Murray, 2015), 33.

22 Olive Schreiner, *From Man to Man*, ed. Dorothy Driver (Cape Town: UCT Press, 2015), 423.

23 Henry Thoreau, *Walking* (Boston: Beacon Press, 1991), 95.

Chapter 2

1 Chris Mann, 'The Rivers', in *New Shades* (Cape Town: David Philip, 1982), 36–7.

2 Penny Bernard, 'Messages from the Deep: Water Divinities, Dreams and Diviners in Southern Africa' (PhD thesis, Rhodes University, 2010), 256.

3 Chris Mann, 'The Poetry of Belonging: Episodic Memory and the Shades' (Unpublished paper, 2012), 12.

4 Elizabeth Bishop, 'The Riverman', in *The Complete Poems 1927–1971* (New York: The Harvest Press, Farrar, Straus and Giroux, 1991), 105.

5 Manton Hirst, 'A River of Metaphors', in *Culture and the Commonplace*, ed. Patrick McAllister (Johannesburg: Wits University Press, 1997), 219.

6 Hirst, 'A River of Metaphors', 234.

7 Tony Dold and Michelle Cooks, *Voices from the Forest: Celebrating Nature and Culture in Xhosaland* (Johannesburg: Jacana Media, 2012), 88.

8 Bernard, 'Messages from the Deep', 40.

9 Dold and Cocks, *Voices from the Forest*, 171. Joan McGregor, in *Crossing the Zambezi* (Oxford: James Currey, 2009), warns about essentialised notions of the connections between people, land and indigenous culture.

10 Robert Godfrey, *Bird Lore of the Eastern Cape Province* (Johannesburg: Wits University Press, 1941), 32.

11 Michelle Cocks, Tony Dold and Sue Vetter, 'God Is My Forest: Xhosa Cultural Values Provide Untapped Opportunities for Conservation', *South African Journal of Science* 108, 5/6 (2012), 52–9.

12 Cocks, Dold and Vetter, 'God Is My Forest', 56.

13 Cocks, Dold and Vetter, 'God Is My Forest', 12.

14 Interview with Dr Jim Cambray, director of the Albany Museum, Grahamstown, 22 December 2005.

15 Yvonne Nakalo Nsubuga, 'Towards Sustainable Utilisation of the Fishery Resources of the Kowie Estuary, South Africa' (MA thesis, Rhodes University, 2014), 8.

16 Brian Goble and Rudy van der Elst, 'The Value of Coastal Ecological Infrastructure', *Environment* 1 (Autumn 2014), 32.

17 Paul Cowley and Craig Daniel, *Review of Estuaries in the Ndlambe Coastal Region*, Report no. 229 (Pietermaritzburg: Institute of Natural Resources, 2001), 19.

18 Interview with Dr Nadine Strydom, Nelson Mandela Metropolitan University, Port Elizabeth, 27 December 2012.

19 Interview with Professor Kate Rowntree, Grahamstown, 4 September 2010.

20 Tom Mullins, 'Grahamstown's Water Supply: A Brief History, 1812 to 2008' (Grahamstown: Kowie Catchment Campaign, 2009), 2.

21 Dold and Cocks, *Voices from the Forest*, 11.

22 Dold and Cocks, *Voices from the Forest*, 12.

23 William Beinart and Luvuyo Wotshela, *Prickly Pear: The Social History of a Plant in the Eastern Cape* (Johannesburg: Wits University Press, 2011).

24 There is a marvellous drawing of this creature in Roy Lubke and Irene de Moor, *Field Guide to the Eastern and Southern Cape Coasts* (Cape Town: University of Cape Town Press, 1988).

25 Donald Moodie, *The Record, or A Series of Official Papers Relative to the Condition and Treatment of the Native Tribes of South Africa* (Cape Town: Murray and St Leger, 1888), 62.

26 John Campbell, *Travels in South Africa*, vol. 1 (Cape Town: Struik, 1974), 107.

27 Cited by Jack Skead, *Historical Mammal Incidence in the Cape Province*, vol. 2 (Cape Town: Chief Directorate of Nature Conservation; Port Elizabeth: Nelson Mandela Metropolitan University, 2007), 730.

28 Campbell, *Travels in South Africa*, 111.

29 Skead, *Historical Mammal Incidence*, 550.

30 Thomas Pringle, *Narrative of a Residence in South Africa* (Cape Town: Struik, 1966), 108.

31 Eric Morse Jones, *The Lower Albany Chronicle, Part 3: 1841–1850* (Port Alfred: Port Alfred Historical Society, 1968), 38.

32 Skead, *Historical Mammal Incidence*, 78.

33 Robert Macfarlane, *The Wild Places* (London: Granta, 2009), 307.

34 Ted Hughes, 'An Otter', in *Lupercal* (London: Faber and Faber, 1960), 91.

35 Isobel Dixon's 'She Comes Swimming', in *Weather Eye* (Cape Town: Carapace Poets, 2001), 13, is a marvellous description of sea otters.

36 Miriam Darlington, *Otter Country: In Search of the Wild Otter* (London: Granta, 2012), 140.

37 Interview with Fred Tyson, pineapple farmer, Lushington, 12 December 2014.

38 Letter from Mike Powell to the author, 4 September 1997.

39 Nsubuga, 'Towards Sustainable Utilisation of the Fishery Resources of the Kowie Estuary', 198.

40 Biff Todd, *The Kowie River* (Port Alfred: Kowie Museum, n.d.), 5.

41 T.S. Eliot, *Four Quartets* (New York: Houghton Mifflin and Harcourt Publishing, 1968).

42 Hermann Giliomee, 'The Eastern Frontier 1770–1812', in *The Shaping of South African Society, 1652–1820*, ed. Richard Elphick and Hermann Giliomee (Cape Town: Longman, 1979), 293.

43 Jeff Peires, 'The Other Side of the Black Silk Handkerchief', *Quarterly Bulletin of the National Library of South Africa* 62 (2008), 9–33.

44 Jeff Guy, 'Ecological Factors in the Rise of Shaka and the Zulu Kingdom,' in *Economy and Society in Pre-industrial South Africa*, ed. Shula Marks and Anthony Atmore (London: Longmans, 1980), 105.

45 Hazel Crampton, Jeff Peires and Carl Vernon, eds, Introduction to *Into the Hitherto Unknown: Ensign Beutler's Expedition to the Eastern Cape, 1752* (Cape Town: Van Riebeeck Society, 2013), v.

46 Clifton Crais, *The Making of the Colonial Order: White Supremacy and Black Resistance in the Eastern Cape 1770–1865* (Johannesburg: Wits University Press, 1992), 18.

47 Robert J. Gordon, *Cape Travels, 1777 to 1786*, vol. 1, ed. Peter Raper and Maurice Boucher (Johannesburg: Brenthurst Press, 1988), 140.

48 Pringle, *Narrative of a Residence*, 268.

49 Timothy Keegan, *Dr Philip's Empire: One Man's Struggle for Justice in Nineteenth-Century South Africa* (Cape Town: Zebra Press, 2016), 79.

50 Jeff Peires, *The House of Phalo: A History of the Xhosa people in the Days of Their Independence* (Johannesburg: Ravan Press, 1981), 2.

51 John Barrow, *An Account of Travels into the Interior of Southern Africa in the Years 1797 and 1798*, vol. 1 (London: T. Cadell and W. Davies, 1801), 111.

52 Barrow, *An Account of Travels*, 180.

53 Peires, *The House of Phalo*, 7.

54 Giliomee, 'The Eastern Frontier', 303.

55 Julie Wells, *The Return of Makhanda: Exploring the Legend* (Pietermaritzburg: UKZN Press, 2012), 79.

56 George Thompson, *Travels and Adventures in Southern Africa*, vol. 1 (London: Henry Colburn, 1827), 192.

57 Jeff Peires, 'An Early History of the Zuurveld', *The Toposcope* 51 (2010), 68.

58 Wells, *The Return of Makhanda*, 92.

59 Cited in Wells, *The Return of Makhanda*, 93.

60 Morse Jones, *The Lower Albany Chronicle, Part 1: 1806–1825*, 4–18.

61 Gavin Menzies, *1421: The Year China Discovered the World* (London: Bantam Books, 2003), 128.

62 Phillip Coates, 'They Built Castles at the Cape', *Cape Argus*, 22 March 1952.

63 Hazel Crampton, *The Sunburnt Queen* (Johannesburg: Jacana Media, 2004), 77, citing Theal, *History of South Africa from 1795 to 1872*.

64 P.R. Kirby, *A Source Book on the Wreck of the Grosvenor* (Cape Town: Van Riebeeck Society, 1953), 109.

65 Kirby, *A Source Book on the Wreck of the Grosvenor*, 112.

66 August Beutler, *Into the Hitherto Unknown: Ensign Beutler's Expedition to the Eastern Cape, 1752* (Cape Town: Van Riebeeck Society, 2013), 71.

67 Beutler, *Into the Hitherto Unknown*, 117.

68 Gordon, *Cape Travels*, 140.

69 François Le Vaillant, *Travels in Africa*, vol. 1 (London: Johnson Reprint, 1972), 353.

70 Le Vaillant, *Travels in Africa*, 353.

71 Vernon Forbes, *Pioneer Travellers in South Africa* (Cape Town: Balkema, 1965), 74.

72 Barrow cited in Forbes, *Pioneer Travellers*, 133

73 Barrow, *An Account of Travels*, 181.

74 Barrow, *An Account of Travels*, 169.

75 Barrow, *An Account of Travels*, 151.

76 Barrow, *An Account of Travels*, 406.

77 Barrow, *An Account of Travels*, 144.

78 Barrow, *An Account of Travels*, 186.

79 Barrow, *An Account of Travels*, 187.

80 Barrow, *An Account of Travels*, 188.

81 Barrow, *An Account of Travels*, 188.

82 Collins, cited in Moodie, *The Record*, 19.

83 Eve Palmer, *The Plains of Camdeboo* (Johannesburg: Penguin Random House, 1996), 53.

84 William Dicey, *Borderline* (Cape Town: Kwela Books, 2004), 206.

85 William Burchell, *Travels in the Interior of South Africa*, vol. 1 (Cape Town: Struik, 1967), 42.

86 Susan Buchanan, *Burchell's Travels: The Art and Journals of William John Burchell 1781–1863* (Johannesburg: Penguin Books, 2015), 178.

87 Campbell, *Travels in South Africa*, 109.

88 Thompson, *Travels and Adventures*, 18.

89 Thompson, *Travels and Adventures*, 22.

90 Thompson, *Travels and Adventures*, 431.

Chapter 3

1 Eddie Diale, 'Makana', *Sechaba* (December 1979), 1.
2 Thomas Willshire, 'The Battle of Grahamstown', *Graham's Town Journal*, 26 September 1846.
3 Charles L. Stretch, *The Journal of Charles Lennox Stretch*, ed. Basil Le Cordeur (Cape Town: Maskew Miller, 1988), 300.
4 Jeff Peires, *The House of Phalo: A History of the Xhosa People in the Days of Their Independence* (Johannesburg: Ravan Press, 1981), 144.
5 Noël Mostert, *Frontiers: The Epic of South Africa's Creation and the Tragedy of the Xhosa People* (New York: Knopf, 1992), 478.
6 Julie Wells, *The Return of Makhanda: Exploring the Legend* (Pietermaritzburg: UKZN Press, 2012), 176.
7 Wells, *The Return of Makhanda*, 39.
8 Stephen Kay, *Travels and Researches in Caffraria* (London: John Mason, 1833), 267.
9 Stretch, *Journal*, 3.
10 Mostert, *Frontiers*, 479. Wells, in *Rebellion and Uproar: Makhanda and the Great Escape from Robben Island, 1820* (Pretoria: Unisa Press, 2007), 179, maintains: 'The battle marked a turning point in African encounters with Europeans which would ripple through the history of the continent for another century.'
11 Peires, *The House of Phalo*, 136–7.
12 Stretch, *Journal*, 12.
13 Donald Moodie, *The Record, or A Series of Official Papers Relative to the Condition and Treatment of the Native Tribes of South Africa* (Cape Town: Murray and St Leger, 1888), 199.
14 Wells, *The Return of Makhanda*, 251.
15 George M. Theal, *History of South Africa from 1795 to 1872*, vol. 1 (London: Allen and Unwin, 1927), 336.
16 Theal, *History of South Africa*, 329.
17 Wells, *The Return of Makhanda*, 253.
18 George Cory, *The Rise of South Africa: From 1820 to 1834*, vol. 2 (Cape Town: Struik, 1965), 383.
19 Thomas Pringle, *Narrative of a Residence in South Africa* (Cape Town: Struik, 1966), 283.
20 Chris Ferree, 'South Africa: More than Zulus and Boers. The Cape Frontier Wars, Part 1' (2005), http://www/geocities.com/cdferee/h/cape wars, 5.
21 Wells, *The Return of Makhanda*, 200.
22 Stretch, *Journal*, 300.
23 Pringle, *Narrative of a Residence*, 288.
24 Wells, *Rebellion and Uproar*, 4.

25 Peires, *House of Phalo*, 65.
26 Ben Maclennan, *A Proper Degree of Terror: John Graham and the Cape Eastern Frontier* (Johannesburg: Ravan Press, 1986), 112.
27 Pringle, *Narrative of a Residence*, 275.
28 Pringle, *Narrative of a Residence*, 274.
29 Maclennan, *A Proper Degree of Terror*, 118.
30 Cory, *Rise of South Africa*, 244.
31 Mostert, *Frontiers*, 392.
32 Pringle, *Narrative of a Residence*, 275.
33 Maclennan, *A Proper Degree of Terror*, 131.
34 Kay, *Travels and Researches*, 254.
35 John Campbell, *Travels in South Africa* (Cape Town: Struik, 1974), 137.
36 Mbeki, cited in *The Star*, 26 May 2005.
37 Robert Macfarlane, *The Wild Places* (London: Granta, 2009), 119.
38 John Bond, *They Were South Africans* (Cape Town: Oxford University Press, 1971), 30.
39 www.ndlambe.co.za, accessed 14 December 2002.
40 Wells, *Return of Makhanda*, 248.
41 Mostert, *Frontiers*, 466.
42 Pringle, *Narrative of a Residence*, 278.
43 Theal, *History of South Africa*, 189.
44 Mostert, *Frontiers*, 270.
45 Collins, in Moodie, *The Record*, 50.
46 Collins, in Moodie, *The Record*, 14.
47 Cory, *Rise of South Africa*, 242.
48 Mostert, *Frontiers*, 569.
49 Mostert, *Frontiers*, 609.
50 Wells, *The Return of Makhanda*, 12.
51 John Galbraith, *Reluctant Empire: British Policy on the South African Frontier, 1834–1854* (Berkeley: University of California Press, 1963), 33.

Chapter 4

1 T.S. Eliot, *Four Quartets* (New York: Houghton Mifflin and Harcourt Publishing,
2 Gleneagles Environmental Consulting, *Environmental Impact Assessment: Scoping Report on the Dredging of the Royal Alfred Marina and Lower Reaches of the Kowie Estuary and Disposal of Soil*, April 2005, 33.
3 Alexis de Tocqueville, *Democracy in America* (New York: Alfred A. Knopf, 1946), 74.
4 Thomas Pringle, *Narrative of a Residence in South Africa* (Cape Town: Struik, 1966), 105.

5   Timothy Keegan, *Colonial South Africa and the Origins of the Racial Order* (Cape Town: David Philip, 1996), 62.

6   Keegan, *Colonial South Africa*, 63.

7   Stephen Kay, *Travels and Researches in Caffraria* (London: John Mason, 1833), 11.

8   Letitia Harriet Cock, 'Reminiscences of Richmond Villa, Kimberley [1946]', MS 14247, Cory Library, Rhodes University.

9   Winifred A. Maxwell and Robert T. McGeogh, eds, *The Reminiscences of Thomas Stubbs, 1814–1876* (Cape Town: Balkema, 1978), 162.

10 Dorothy Rivett-Carnac, *Thus Came the English* (Cape Town: Howard Timmins, 1961), 14.

11 Guy Butler, *The 1820 Settlers: An Illustrated Commentary* (Cape Town: Human and Rousseau, 1974), 221.

12 George Thompson, *Travels and Adventures in Southern Africa*, vol. 1 (London: Henry Colburn, 1827), 423.

13 Jonathan Stead, *The Development and Failure of the Eastern Cape Separatist Movement* (Pretoria: Government Printer, 1984), 49.

14 William Cock, Journal, MS 14262, Cory Library, Rhodes University, 14.

15 Eric Turpin, *Basket Work Harbour: The Story of the Kowie* (Cape Town: Howard Timmins, 1964), 33.

16 L.H. Cock, 'Reminiscences of Richmond Villa', 3.

17 L.H. Cock, 'Reminiscences of Richmond Villa', 3.

18 Eric Tucker, 'The Castle above the Kowie', *Eastern Province Herald*, 12 August 1970, 4.

19 John Bond, *They Were South Africans* (Cape Town: Oxford University Press, 1971), 91.

20 Godlonton, in *Graham's Town Journal*, 2 March 1841.

21 William Cock, Journal, 12.

22 William Cock Letters, MS 14263, Cory Library, Rhodes University, W. Cock to W.F. Cock, 15 March 1852.

23 Turpin, *Basket Work Harbour*, 45.

24 Cited in *Graham's Town Journal*, 4 July 1873.

25 Turpin, *Basket Work Harbour*, 85.

26 William Rose, 'Personal Reminiscences from the 1870s', in *Looking Back at Port Alfred*, ed. Douglas Bailes (Port Alfred: Kowie History Museum, 2006), 9–10.

27 Rose, 'Personal Reminiscences from the 1870s', 25.

28 John Garner, 'Jim's Journal: The Diary of James Butler' (MA thesis, Rhodes University, 1983), 240.

29 Garner, 'Jim's Journal', citing James Butler, 241. This 'swamp' was actually a salt marsh, a type of wetland.

30 Rose, 'Personal Reminiscences from the 1870s', 13.

31 Turpin, *Basket Work Harbour*, 113.

32 Nigel Penn, ' "Close and Merciful Watchfulness": John Montagu's Convict System in the Mid-Nineteenth-Century Cape Colony', *Cultural and Social History* 5, 4 (1980), 465.

33 Letter from the Convict Station Superintendent to the Colonial Secretary, 28 May 1864, CA CO 6287.

34 Turpin, *Basket Work Harbour*, 75.

35 Superintendent of the Kowie Convict Station, 24 March 1859, CA CO 6287.

36 L.H. Cock, 'Reminiscences of Richmond Villa'.

37 Stead, *The Development and Failure of the Eastern Cape Separatist Movement*, 48.

38 Basil Le Cordeur, *The Politics of Eastern Cape Separatism* (Cape Town: Oxford University Press, 1981), 219.

39 Biff Todd, *The Kowie River* (Port Alfred: Kowie Museum, n.d.), 5.

40 Rose, 'Personal Reminiscences from the 1870s', 10.

41 Stead, *The Development and Failure of the Eastern Cape Separatist Movement*, 49.

42 Roger Beck, 'Bibles and Beads: Missionaries as Raiders in Southern Africa in the Early Nineteenth Century', *Journal of African History* 30, 2 (1989), 223.

43 The value of the original shares rose from £16 13s 4d to £42 in a few years.

44 Godlonton, in *Graham's Town Journal*, 11 February 1876.

45 Keegan, *Colonial South Africa*, 285.

46 Stead, *The Development and Failure of the Eastern Cape Separatist Movement*, 48.

47 Le Cordeur, *The Politics of Eastern Cape Separatism*, 281.

48 Alan F. Hattersley, *The Convict Crisis and the Growth of Unity* (Pietermaritzburg: UKZN Press, 1965), 55.

49 Rivett-Carnac, *Thus Came the English*, 127.

50 Ely Gledhill, 'William Cock: A Pioneer of Commerce', *Africana Notes and News* 14, 3 (September 1960), 87.

51 Stanley Trapido, 'The Origins of the Cape Franchise Qualification', *Journal of African History* 5, 1 (1964), 51.

52 Le Cordeur, *The Politics of Eastern Cape Separatism*, 219.

53 L.H. Cock, 'Reminiscences of Richmond Villa', 3.

54 Pamela Anderson, 'The Human Clay: An Essay in the Spatial History of the Cape Eastern Frontier, 1811–1835' (MLitt, University of Oxford, 1993), 17.

55 William Cock, Journal, 5 May, 1846.

56 Michael Berning, ed., *The Historical Conversations of Sir George Cory* (Cape Town: Maskew Miller Longman, 1989), 163.

57 Clifton Crais, *The Making of the Colonial Order: White Supremacy and Black Resistance in the Eastern Cape 1770–1865* (Johannesburg: Wits University Press, 1992), 191, citing Southey to Godlonton, 11 December 1850.
58 Keegan, *Colonial South Africa*, 145.
59 Maxwell and McGeogh, *The Reminiscences of Thomas Stubbs*, 136.
60 Jeff Peires, *The House of Phalo: A History of the Xhosa People in the Days of Their Independence* (Johannesburg: Ravan Press, 1981), 123–4.
61 Keegan, *Colonial South Africa*, 136.

Chapter 5

1 Mary Oliver (1935–), *Upstream: Selected Essays* (New York: Penguin Press, 2016), 4.
2 Port Alfred Municipality, *Sunday Times*, 11 January 1987.
3 Don Pinnock, *The Woman Who Lived in a Tree* (Johannesburg: Jacana Media, 2009), 283.
4 Conversation with marina developer, Port Alfred, 15 December 2015.
5 Steyn, cited in *Talk of the Town*, commemorative edition, 23 October 2014.
6 Plan Associates, 'Port Alfred Environmental Impact Assessment: Phase 2, Marina and Small Craft Harbour Impacts', 1986, 53.
7 Letter from Professor Roy Lubke in *Talk of the Town*, 17 December 2015.
8 Interview with Professor Lubke, Grahamstown, 15 December 2016.
9 *Kowie Announcer*, 29 July 1988.
10 Gleneagles Environmental Consulting, *Environmental Impact Assessment: Draft Scoping Report on the Dredging of the Royal Alfred Marina and Lower Reaches of the Kowie Estuary and Disposal of Soil*, March 2005, 23.
11 Memorandum of Agreement (MOA), vol. 1, 10, Port Alfred Marina archives.
12 MOA, vol. 1, 6.
13 Letter from Louise Swanepoel in *Talk of the Town*, 13 December 2012.
14 MOA, vol. 1, 22.
15 Cited in *Talk of the Town*, 23 October 2014.
16 Interview with local estate agent, 7 August 2016.
17 Interview with town planner, Port Alfred, 2 October 2016.
18 Interview with ecologist, Port Alfred, 6 December 2015.
19 Interview with Angus Schlemmer, marina manager, Port Alfred, 11 December 2015.
20 *Kowie Announcer*, 27 January 1989.
21 *Talk of the Town*, 20 February 2014.
22 Gleneagles Environmental Consulting, *Environmental Impact Assessment: Scoping Report on the Dredging of the Royal Port Alfred Marina and Lower Reaches of the Kowie Estuary and Disposal of Soil*, April 2005, 35.

23 Conversation with an informant who was close to the defamation case.

24 Letter to the town clerk of Port Alfred from the assistant advocate-general, 18 April 1988, Port Alfred Marina archives.

25 *The Herald*, 28 March 2013.

26 Letter attached to RAMHOA submission to DEDEAT, 2015.

27 Email communication to Angus Schlemmer, 30 December 2016.

28 Letter in *Talk of the Town*, 31 March 2006.

29 Gleneagles Environmental Consulting, *Environmental Impact Assessment*, April 2005, 15.

30 Conversation with an informant who is a longstanding resident of Port Alfred.

31 Statistics South Africa, 'General Household Survey 2015' (Pretoria, 2015), 59.

32 Gleneagles Environmental Consulting, *Environmental Impact Assessment*, March 2005, 15.

33 J.L.B. Smith, *The Sea Fishes of Southern Africa* (Johannesburg: Central News Agency, 1950), 162.

34 Interview with marine biologist, Nelson Mandela Metropolitan University, 28 December 2012.

35 Brian Davies and Jenny Day, *Vanishing Waters* (Cape Town: UCT Press, 1988), 37.

36 Angus Paterson, 'Salt Marshes: Jewels of the Eastern Cape', *Eastern Cape Estuaries Management Programme Newsletter* 4 (Summer 2000), 6.

37 Muller Coetzee, 'Our Coast of Opportunity and Challenges', *African Wildlife* 50, 1 (2015), 8.

38 Gleneagles Environmental Consulting, *Environmental Impact Assessment*, April 2005, 1.

39 Paul Cowley and Craig Daniel, *Review of Estuaries in the Ndlambe Coastal Region*, Report no. 229 (Pietermaritzburg: Institute of Natural Resources, 2001), 3.

40 Gleneagles Environmental Consulting, *Environmental Impact Assessment*, April 2005, 12.

41 Gleneagles Environmental Consulting, *Environmental Impact Assessment*, April 2005, 33.

42 Duncan Hay, 'Dredging Estuaries', *Eastern Cape Management Programme Newsletter* 4 (2000), 7.

43 Gleneagles Environmental Consulting, *Environmental Impact Assessment*, April 2005, 20.

44 *Talk of the Town*, 6 June 2013.

45 Interview, Port Alfred, 12 January 2016.

46 Gleneagles Environmental Consulting, *Environmental Impact Assessment*, April 2005, 65.

47 Letter to the municipal manager of Ndlambe and Shepstone & Wylie Attorneys, 16 November 2015.

48 Interview with environmentalist, Port Elizabeth, 8 February 2016.

49 *Talk of the Town*, 3 December 2015.

50 *Talk of the Town*, 3 December 2015.

51 Conversation with a government official.

52 Open letter to the Director of the Port Elizabeth office of DEDEAT, published in *Talk of the Town*, 7 April 2006.

53 *Talk of the Town*, 25 December 2014.

54 *Talk of the Town*, 16 April 2015.

55 *Talk of the Town*, 7 April 2016.

56 Ndlambe Municipality, 'Integrated Development Plan 2012-2017: Draft Review 2016-2017', 2016, 40.

57 Simon du Toit and James Taylor, 'Water Resources and Social Change', *Environment, People and Conservation in Africa* 9 (2011), 8.

58 Interview with project manager.

59 Interview with Enoch Jobela, municipal official, Port Alfred, 11 January 2015.

60 Interview with Dr Jim Cambray, then director of the Albany Museum, Grahamstown, 22 December 2005.

61 Interview with Dr Jim Cambray, 22 December 2005.

Chapter 6

1 Damian Short, *Redefining Genocide: Settler Colonialism, Social Death and Ecocide* (London: Zed Books, 2016), 6.

2 Martin Legassick, 'The State, Racism and the Rise of Capitalism in the Nineteenth-Century Cape Colony', *South African Historical Journal* 28 (1993), 354.

3 Stubbs, in *The Reminiscences of Thomas Stubbs, 1814-1876*, ed. Winifred A. Maxwell and Robert T. McGeogh (Cape Town: Balkema, 1978), 135.

4 Ngũgĩ wa Thiong'o, interview by Mohdi Ganjavi, Toronto, reported in *Pambazuka News*, 20 April 2017.

5 Anna Orthofer, 'Wealth Inequality in South Africa', Working Paper 15, Research Project on Employment, Income Distribution and Inclusive Growth, University of Cape Town, 2016, 4.

6 Bev Young, in *Talk of the Town*, 23 October 2014.

7 Interview with local farmer, fourth-generation 1820 settler descendant, Port Alfred, 2 December 2013.

8 Lorenzo Veracini, *Settler Colonialism: A Theoretical Overview* (London: Palgrave Macmillan, 2010), 95.

9 *Graham's Town Journal*, 19 August 1919.

10 Anna Tsing, *The Mushroom at the End of the World: On the Possibility of Life in Capitalist Ruins* (Princeton: Princeton University Press, 2015), 5.

11 Anthony Turton, cited in *The Star*, 11 December 2015.

12 Kerry Cullinan, 'Our Most Precious Resource under Threat', *The Star*, 5 May 2016.

13 Sheree Bega, 'Clearing the Muddy Waters', *Saturday Star*, 11 January 2014.

14 Alan Whitfield, 'Are We Looking After Our Estuaries?' *Environment, People and Conservation in Africa* 9 (2011), 8–9.

15 J.K. Turpie, 'Assessment of the Conservation Priority Status of South African Estuaries for Use in Management and Water Allocation', *Water SA* 28, 2 (April 2002), 200.

16 Yvonne Nakalo Nsubuga, 'Towards Sustainable Utilisation of the Fishery Resources of the Kowie Estuary, South Africa' (MA thesis, Rhodes University, 2014), 21.

17 Jacklyn Cock, 'Challenging Environmental Injustice and Inequality in Contemporary South Africa', in *New South African Review 6*, ed. Gilbert Khadiagala, Sarah Mosoetsa, Devan Pillay and Roger Southall (Johannesburg: Wits University Press, 2018).

18 Hilary Wainwright, *The Tragedy of the Private, the Potential of the Public* (London: Transnational Institute, Public Services International, 2014), 4.

19 David Lindley, 'Recent Floods a Reminder of the Importance of Wetlands', *Environment, People and Conservation in Africa* 6 (Autumn 2011), 6.

20 Brian Davies and Jenny Day, *Vanishing Waters* (Cape Town: UCT Press, 1988), 38.

21 Samantha Stelli, 'Wetlands: Essential Ecosystem That Requires Our Protection', *Environment, People and Conservation in Africa* 12 (Spring 2012), 21.

22 International Rivers Network, Statement, 14 March 2008.

23 David Still, in *Mail & Guardian*, 27 February 2014.

24 Wildlife and Environment Society of South Africa (WESSA) statement, 20 October 2015.

25 Jim Cambray, in *Talk of the Town*, 17 June 2005.

26 Eddie Koch, 'Rainbow Alliances', in *Going Green: People, Politics and the Environment in South Africa*, ed. Jacklyn Cock and Eddie Koch (Cape Town: Oxford University Press, 1991), 27.

27 WoMin, *No Longer a Life Worth Living* (Johannesburg: WoMin, 2016), iii.

28 Raymond Williams, *Keywords* (Harmondsworth: Penguin, 1980), 219.

29 Susan George, 'Committing Geocide: Climate Change and Corporate Capture', Paper delivered at the International Centre for the Promotion of Human Rights', Buenos Aires, 1–2 September 2016.

30 Cited in Jonathan Wiener, *The Beak of the Finch* (New York: Vintage Books, 1995), 281.

31 Robert Macfarlane, *The Wild Places* (London: Granta, 2009), 203.

32 Miriam Darlington, *Otter Country: In Search of the Wild Otter* (London: Granta, 2012), 132.

33 Sindiswa Nobula, in *Mail & Guardian*, 27 July 2014.

34 Christopher D. Stone, *Should Trees Have Standing? Law, Morality and the Environment*, 3rd edn (New York: Oxford University Press, 2010).

35 https://voices.nationalgeographic.org?2012/09/04/a-river-in-NewZealand-gets-a-legal-status.

36 Conversation with Cormac Cullinan, Cape Town, July 2016.

37 Jacklyn Cock and David Fig, 'From Colonial to Community Based Conservation: Environmental Justice and the National Parks of South Africa', *Society in Transition* 31, 1 (2000), 23.

38 Glen Coulthard, *Red Skin, White Masks: Rejecting the Colonial Politics of Recognition* (Minneapolis: University of Minnesota Press, 2014), 13.

39 Nokulinda Mkhize, 'Of Black People and Nature', *City Press*, 10 February 2013; Michelle Cocks, Tony Dold and Sue Vetter, 'God Is My Forest: Xhosa Cultural Values Provide Untapped Opportunities for Conservation', *South African Journal of Science* 108, 5/6 (2012), 52–9.

40 Aldo Leopold, *A Sand County Almanac* (New York: Ballantine Books, 1966), 224–5.

41 Barry Lopez, 'The Language of Animals', *Wild Earth* 8, 2 (Summer 1998), 5.

42 Annie Proulx, *Bird Cloud: A Memoir of Place* (London: Fourth Estate, 2012), 169.

43 Davies and Day, *Vanishing Waters*, 79.

44 Don Pinnock, 'Damn Dams', watercaucus@googlegroups.com, accessed 13 May 2014.

45 Gleneagles Environmental Consulting, *Environmental Impact Assessment: Scoping Report on the Dredging of the Royal Port Alfred Marina and Lower Reaches of the Kowie Estuary and Disposal of Soil*, April 2005, 64.

46 Thiven Reddy, *South Africa, Settler Colonialism and the Failures of Liberal Democracy* (Johannesburg: Wits University Press, 2016), 136.

47 Tsing, *The Mushroom at the End of the World*, 262.

48 William Fiennes, *The Snow Goose* (Harmondsworth: Penguin, 2002), 106.

49 Barry Lopez, 'The Language of Animals', *Wild Earth* 8, 2 (Summer 1998), 5.

50 Vandana Shiva, *Making Peace with the Earth: Beyond Resource, Land and Food Wars* (New Delhi: Women Unlimited, 2012; Johannesburg: Jacana Media, 2013), 11.

Glossary of isiXhosa terms

Meanings provided here derive from the author's reading of the research texts consulted for this project.

Abantu Bomlambo	the People of the River
amagqirha	healers or diviners
amalinde	pits or depressions created by giant earthworms
Egazini	the 'place of blood', marking the Battle of Grahamstown in 1819
Emqwashini	the site of the Mfengu meeting with the Cape governor in 1835
impila	health and well-being
indalo	nature
intaba izono	the mountain of danger
intini	otters
intlwayalelo	initiation ritual for a diviner or healer
intsila	body dirt of candidate diviners
inyanga	diviner
iqhilika	drink made from prickly pears
itolofiya	prickly pears
izithunywa	messengers from the ancestors
ubuhlanti	a holding pen for animals
ukuhlupeza	fierce warrior
umkwetha	candidate diviner or healer
umqwashu	milkwood tree
umthombo	spring of water
uqhimngqofe	Hamerkop bird

List of Figures

sandbars, which meant extreme variations in the level of the water as the tides changed. He established that at the river mouth tides rose suffciently to admit vessels of up to about 120 tons (Cory Library/Rhodes University).

9. William Cock (1793–1876), the author's great-great-grandfather seen here in 1864, was principally responsible for the development of the harbour at the mouth of the Kowie River, beginning in 1838 (Cock Family Archive).

10. William Cock was appointed to the Cape Legislative Council in 1847, where he worked to promote the expansion of the colony, which involved the dispossession of the Xhosa, and to secure the governor's support for the harbour project. He is seen here (back right) with other members of the Council in 1864 (Cock Family Archive).

11. Under Cock's direction a new mouth was cut for the river through the sand hills of the west bank. The river was canalised and the channel straightened and diverted to the western side of the estuary, producing a navigable stretch of about three-quarters of a mile inland (Date of photograph unknown. Western Cape Archives, AG 1443).

12. Sedimentation was a problem, so to keep the river mouth deep enough, two piers were built in the 1850s extending into the sea. The estuary was regularly dredged to allow the velocity of the tide to flush the mouth and keep the harbour free of sand (Date of photograph unknown. Cory Library/Africa Media Online).

13. Throughout the 1840s the harbour was used by sailing ships, usually small schooners and cutters. Their cargoes were partially offloaded into small boats before they attempted to enter the river. Locally built lighters were used to unload larger vessels anchored out at sea (Date of photograph unknown. Cory Library/Africa Media Online).

14. The Albany Steam Navigation Company, owned by William Cock, operated the *Sir John St Aubyn*, an iron steamship for cargo and passengers that made its first journey from Cape Town to Port Frances (later Port Alfred) in record time ($3^1/_2$ days) in July 1842 (Painting by Edith Cock, 1840s. Cock Family Archive).

15. Steamship moored in the Kowie River. The harbour development increased trade between the port, Cape Town, England and Mauritius. Ships took cargoes of sheep, butter, beans, grain, hide and tallow to Mauritius and brought back sugar. The harbour was busiest in the 1870s with 101 ships entering in 1876 (Date of photograph unknown. Western Cape Archives, AG 4651).

16. View of the Kowie River by Thomas Bowler, from the flagpole in front of William Cock's house, according to a family member. The view shows the dredger at work in the river (Hand-coloured engraving from original artwork by Thomas Bowler, 1864. Cory Library/Africa Media Online).

29. Overview of the Royal Alfred Marina developed at the mouth of the Kowie River in 1989 by a private developer (Photograph: David Stott).
30. Looking across towards the East Bank. The marina destroyed a wetland, privatised a public asset, and causes ongoing silting in the Kowie River (Photograph: Joanna Rice).
31. The marina consists of 355 upmarket houses each with its own waterfront. They are mostly holiday homes for wealthy upcountry visitors (Photograph: David Stott).
32. Nemato township, Port Alfred. An 8 km walk to the town centre, this is home to thousands of Africans living with high rates of poverty, unemployment, hunger, and uneven and irregular provision of municipal services (Photograph: David Larsen/Africa Media Online).

Bibliography

Published works

Agrawal, Arun, and Clark Gibson. 'Enchantment and Disenchantment: The Role of Community in Natural Resource Conservation'. *World Development* 27, 4 (1999): 629–649.

Albinia, Alice. *Empires of the Indus: The Story of a River*. London: John Murray, 1988.

'A Little Girl Gave Port Alfred Name'. *Eastern Province Herald*, 10 October 1987.

Anderson, Clare. *Subaltern Lives: Biographies of Colonialism in the Indian Ocean World 1790–1920*. Cambridge: Cambridge University Press, 2012.

Anderson, Pamela. 'The Human Clay: An Essay in the Spatial History of the Cape Eastern Frontier, 1811–1835'. MLitt, University of Oxford, 1993.

Bailes, Douglas. *Looking Back at Port Alfred*. Port Alfred: The Kowie History Museum, 2006.

Barrow, John. *An Account of Travels into the Interior of Southern Africa in the years 1797 and 1798*, vol. 1. London: T. Cadell and W. Davies, 1801.

Beck, Roger. 'Bibles and Beads: Missionaries as Raiders in Southern Africa in the Early Nineteenth Century'. *Journal of African History* 30, 2 (1989): 211–225.

Bega, Sheree. 'Clearing the Muddy Waters'. *Saturday Star*, 11 January 2014.

Beinart, William, and Luvuyo Wotshela. *Prickly Pear: The Social History of a Plant in the Eastern Cape*. Johannesburg: Wits University Press, 2011.

Berkes, Fikret. *Sacred Ecology*, 2nd edn. New York: Routledge, 2008.

Bernard, Penny. 'Messages from the Deep: Water Divinities, Dreams and Diviners in Southern Africa'. PhD thesis, Rhodes University, 2010.

Bernard, Penny. 'Sacred Water Sites and Indigenous Healers in Southern Africa: The Need to Protect Knowledge, Nature and Resource Rights'. Paper presented at Indigenous Knowledge conference, Port Elizabeth, 2001.

Berning, Michael, ed. *The Historical Conversations of Sir George Cory*. Cape Town: Maskew Miller Longman, 1989.

Beutler, August. *Into the Hitherto Unknown: Ensign Beutler's Expedition to the Eastern Cape 1752*. Cape Town: Van Riebeeck Society, 2013.

Bishop, Elizabeth. 'The Riverman'. In *The Complete Poems 1927–1971*. New York: The Harvest Press, Farrar, Straus and Giroux, 1991.

Bond, John. *They Were South Africans*. Cape Town: Oxford University Press, 1971.

Bradford, Helen, 'Highways, Byways and Cul-de-Sacs: The Transition to Agrarian Capitalism in Revisionist South Africa'. *Radical History Review* 46, 7 (1990): 59–88.

Branford, Jean, and William Branford. *A Dictionary of South African English*. Oxford: Oxford University Press, 1980.

Buchanan, Susan. *Burchell's Travels: The Art and Journals of William John Burchell 1781–1863*. Johannesburg: Penguin Books, 2015.

Burchell, William. *Travels in the Interior of South Africa*, vol. 1. Cape Town: Struik, 1967 [1822].

Butler, Guy. *The 1820 Settlers: An Illustrated Commentary*. Cape Town: Human and Rousseau, 1974.

Cambray, Jim. *Kowie River, Home of the Endangered Eastern Cape Rocky*. Grahamstown: Albany Museum, 2004.

Campbell, John, *Travels in South Africa*. Cape Town: Struik, 1974 [1815].

Clement, Andrew J. 'History in the Kowie Dunes'. *The Toposcope* 17 (1986): 73–76.

Coates, Phillip. 'They Built Castles at the Cape'. *Cape Argus*, 22 March 1952.

Cock, Jacklyn. 'Challenging Environmental Injustice and Inequality in Contemporary South Africa'. In *New South African Review 6*, edited by Gilbert Khadiagala, Sarah Mosoetsa, Devan Pillay and Roger Southall, 252–267. Johannesburg, Wits University Press, 2018.

Cock, Jacklyn. 'Connecting the Red, Brown and Green: The Environmental Justice Movement in South Africa'. In *Voices of Protest: Social Movements in Post-Apartheid South Africa*, edited by Richard Ballard, Adam Habib and Imraan Valodia, 203–224. Pietermaritzburg: UKZN Press, 2006.

Cock, Jacklyn. 'The "Green Economy": A Just and Sustainable Development Path or a Wolf in Sheep's Clothing.' *Global Labour Journal* 5 (2015): 1–28.

Cock, Jacklyn, and David Fig. 'From Colonial to Community Based Conservation: Environmental Justice and the National Parks of South Africa'. *Society in Transition* 31, 1 (2000): 22–35.

Cocks, Michelle. 'Biocultural Diversity: Moving beyond the Realm of "Indigenous" and "Local" People'. *Human Ecology* 10 (2006): 59–76.

Cocks, Michelle, Tony Dold and Sue Vetter. 'God Is My Forest: Xhosa Cultural Values Provide Untapped Opportunities for Conservation'. *South African Journal of Science* 108, 5/6 (2012): 52–59.

Coetzee, Muller. 'Our Coast of Opportunity and Challenges'. *African Wildlife* 50, 1 (2015): 8–10.

Collins, Robert O. *The Nile*. New Haven: Yale University Press, 2002.

Conrad, Joseph. *The Heart of Darkness and Other Stories*. London: Wordsworth Classics, 1995 [1902].

Cory, George. 'Grahamstown'. In *Souvenir in Commemoration of the Centenary of the 1820 Settlers of Albany*. Grahamstown: City Council, 1920.

Cory, George. *The Rise of South Africa*, vol. 2: *From 1820 to 1834*. Cape Town: Struik, 1965 [1910].

Coulthard, Glen. *Red Skin, White Masks: Rejecting the Colonial Politics of Recognition*. Minneapolis: University of Minnesota Press, 2014.

Crais, Clifton. *The Making of the Colonial Order: White Supremacy and Black Resistance in the Eastern Cape 1770–1865*. Johannesburg: Wits University Press, 1992.

Crampton, Hazel. *The Sunburnt Queen*. Johannesburg: Jacana Media, 2004.

Crampton, Hazel, Jeff Peires and Carl Vernon, eds. Introduction to *Into the Hitherto Unknown: Ensign Beutler's Expedition to the Eastern Cape, 1752*. Cape Town: Van Riebeeck Society, 2013.

Crompton, Rod, and Alec Erwin. 'Reds and Greens: Labour and the Environment'. In *Going Green: People, Politics and the Environment in South Africa*, edited by Jacklyn Cock and Eddie Koch, 78–91. Cape Town: Oxford University Press, 1991.

Cullinan, Kerry. 'Our Most Precious Resource under Threat'. *The Star*, 5 May 2016.

Darlington, Miriam. *Otter Country: In Search of the Wild Otter*. London: Granta, 2012.

Davies, Brian, and Jenny Day. *Vanishing Waters*. Cape Town: UCT Press, 1988.

Denoon, Donald. *Settler Capitalism: The Dynamics of Dependent Development in the Southern Hemisphere*. Oxford: Clarendon Press, 1983.

De Waal, Francois. *Are We Smart Enough to Know How Smart Animals Are?* London: Granta, 2016.

Diale, Eddie. 'Makana'. *Sechaba* (December 1979): 3–5.

Dicey, William. *Borderline*. Cape Town: Kwela Books, 2004.

Dixon, Isobel. 'She Comes Swimming'. In *Weather Eye*. Cape Town: Carapace Poets, 2001.

Dold, Tony, and Michelle Cooks. *Voices from the Forest: Celebrating Nature and Culture in Xhosaland*. Johannesburg: Jacana Media, 2012.

Dowling, Patrick. 'Shocking Water Quality'. *African Wildlife* 29, 2 (1994): 11.

'Dredging of Kowie Estuary: Appeal Responding Statement'. *Public Service Accountability Monitor* (August 2015): 1–7.

Dugmore, Henry. *Reminiscences of an Albany Settler*. Grahamstown: Grocott and Sherry, 1958 [1871].

Duminy, Andrew. 'The Role of Sir Andries Stockenström in Cape Politics 1848–1856'. In *Archives Year Book for South African History*, 78–174. Pretoria: Government Printer, 1961.

Du Toit, Simon, and James Taylor. 'Water Resources and Social Change'. *Environment, People and Conservation in Africa* 9 (2011): 30–31.

Eliot, T.S. *Four Quartets, Little Gidding and the Dry Salvages*. New York: Houghton Mifflin and Harcourt Publishing, 1968.

Elphick, Richard, and Hermann Giliomee. *The Shaping of South African Society 1652–1820*. Cape Town: Longmans, 1979.

Erasmus, Mike. 'Silting Problem Goes Back 150 Years'. *Talk of the Town*, 15 June 2007.

Ferree, Chris. 'South Africa: More than Zulus and Boers. The Cape Frontier Wars, Part 1' (2005). http://www/geocities.com/cdferee/h/cape wars, accessed 10 March 2005.

Fiennes, William. *The Snow Goose*. Harmondsworth: Penguin, 2002.

Forbes, Vernon. *Pioneer Travellers in South Africa*. Cape Town: Balkema, 1965.

Galbraith, John. *Reluctant Empire: British Policy on the South African Frontier, 1834–1854*. Berkeley: University of California Press, 1963.

Garner, John. 'Jim's Journal: The Diary of James Butler'. MA thesis, Rhodes University, 1983.

George, Susan. 'Committing Geocide: Climate Change and Corporate Capture'. Paper delivered at the International Centre for the Promotion of Human Rights, Buenos Aires, 1–2 September 2016.

Giliomee, Hermann. 'The Eastern Frontier 1770–1812'. In *The Shaping of South African Society, 1652–1820*, edited by Richard Elphick and Hermann Giliomee, 290–337. Cape Town: Longman, 1979.

Gledhill, Ely. 'William Cock: A Pioneer of Commerce'. *Africana Notes and News* 14, 3 (September 1960): 83–84.

Goble, Brian, and Rudy van der Elst. 'The Value of Coastal Ecological Infrastructure'. *Environment* 1 (Autumn 2014): 28–33.

Godfrey, Robert. *Bird Lore of the Eastern Cape Province*. Johannesburg: Wits University Press, 1941.

Gordon, Robert J. *Cape Travels, 1777 to 1786*, edited by Peter Raper and Maurice Boucher, vol. 1. Johannesburg: Brenthurst Press, 1988.

Gurney, Marie. 'The Business Case for Investment in Ecological Infrastructure'. *Environment* 18 (Autumn 2014): 38–41.

Guy, Jeff. 'Ecological Factors in the Rise of Shaka and the Zulu Kingdom'. In *Economy and Society in Pre-industrial South Africa*, edited by Shula Marks and Anthony Atmore, 102–124. London: Longman, 1980.

Haraway, Donna. 'Situated Knowledge: The Science Question in Feminism and the Privilege of Partial Perspective'. *Feminist Studies* 14, 3 (1988): 575–599.

Hardyment, Christine. 'The Strippling Thames'. *Oxford Today* 24, 3 (2012): 42–43.

Hart, Gill. *Disabling Globalization: Places of Power in Post-apartheid South Africa*. Durban: UKZN Press, 2012.

Hart, Gill. *Rethinking the South African Crisis: Nationalism, Populism, Hegemony*. Durban: UKZN Press, 2013.

Harvey, David. *The Enigma of Capital*. New York: Oxford University Press, 2010.

Harvey, David. *The New Imperialism*. New York: Oxford University Press, 2005.

Harwood, Phil. *Canoeing the Congo*. London: Troubador Publishers, 2012.

Hattersley, Alan F. *The Convict Crisis and the Growth of Unity*. Pietermaritzburg: UKZN Press, 1965.

Hay, Duncan. 'Dredging Estuaries'. *Eastern Cape Management Programme Newsletter* 4 (2000).

Hirst, Manton. 'A River of Metaphors'. In *Culture and the Commonplace*, edited by Patrick McAllister. Johannesburg: Wits University Press, 1997.

Hughes, Ted. 'An Otter'. In *Lupercal*. London: Faber and Faber, 1960.

Hunter, Monica. *Reaction to Conquest: Effects of Contact with Europeans on the Pondo*. Oxford: Oxford University Press, 1936.

Kay, Stephen. *Travels and Researches in Caffraria*. London: John Mason, 1833.

Keegan, Timothy. *Colonial South Africa and the Origins of the Racial Order*. Cape Town: David Philip, 1996.

Keegan, Timothy. *Dr Philip's Empire: One Man's Struggle for Justice in Nineteenth-Century South Africa*. Cape Town: Zebra Press, 2016.

Keegan, Timothy. 'The Origins of Agrarian Capitalism in South Africa'. *Journal of Southern African Studies* 15, 3 (1989): 666–684.

Keegan, Timothy. 'Race, Class and Economic Development in South Africa'. *Social Dynamics* 15, 1 (1989): 111–123.

Kirby, P.R. *A Source Book on the Wreck of the Grosvenor*. Cape Town: Van Riebeeck Society, 1953.

Knowles, Rob. 'In Sewage Trouble'. *Talk of the Town*, 31 December 2010.

Koch, Eddie. 'Rainbow Alliances'. In *Going Green: People, Politics and the Environment in South Africa*, edited by Jacklyn Cock and Eddie Koch, 20–32. Cape Town: Oxford University Press, 1991.

Laganparsad, Monica. 'Millions at Risk from Rivers of Disease'. *Sunday Times*, 29 March 2009.

Laing, Olivia. *To the River: A Journey beneath the Surface*. London: Canongate, 2011.

Le Cordeur, Basil. *The Politics of Eastern Cape Separatism*. Cape Town: Oxford University Press, 1981.

Legassick, Martin. 'The State, Racism and the Rise of Capitalism in the Nineteenth-Century Cape Colony'. *South African Historical Journal* 28 (1993): 329–368.

Legassick, Martin. *The Struggle for the Eastern Cape 1800–1854: Subjugation and the Roots of South African Democracy*. Johannesburg: KMM Review, 2010.

Leopold, Aldo. *A Sand County Almanac*. New York: Ballantine Books, 1966 [1949].

Lerumo, A. 'Fifty Fighting Years: The Communist Party of South Africa 1921–1971'. www.sacp.org.za/docs/history/fifty.html.

Le Vaillant, François. *Travels in Africa*, vol. 1. London: Johnson Reprint Corporation, 1972 [1790].

Lindley, David. 'Recent Floods a Reminder of the Importance of Wetlands'. *Environment, People and Conservation in Africa* 6 (Autumn 2011): 5–11.

Lopez, Barry. 'The Language of Animals'. *Wild Earth* 8, 2 (Summer 1998): 2–6.

Lubke, Roy, and Irene de Moor. *Field Guide to the Eastern and Southern Cape Coasts*. Cape Town: UCT Press, 1988.

Lubke, Roy, Fred Gess and Michael Bruton. *A Field Guide to the Eastern Cape Coast*. Grahamstown: Wildlife Society of Southern Africa, 1988.

Macfarlane, Robert. *The Wild Places*. London: Granta, 2009.

Macgregor, Dave. 'Concern at Kowie Wetland Pollution'. *Eastern Province Herald*, 13 January 2011.

Maclennan, Ben. *A Proper Degree of Terror: John Graham and the Cape Eastern Frontier*. Johannesburg: Ravan Press, 1986.

Mann, Chris, 'The Poetry of Belonging: Episodic Memory and the Shades'. Unpublished paper, 2012.

Mann, Chris. 'The Rivers'. In *New Shades*, 36. Cape Town: David Philip, 1982.

Mann, Chris. 'Tea at Hlambeza's Pool'. In *Heartlands*, 68. Pietermaritzburg: UKZN Press, 2002.

Matshiqi, Aubrey. 'Denial of Unpalatable Truth Is a Road to Nowhere'. *Business Day*, 14 June 2016.

Maxwell, Winifred A., and Robert T. McGeogh, eds. *The Reminiscences of Thomas Stubbs, 1814–1876*. Cape Town: Balkema, 1978.

McCarthy, David. *The Moth Snowstorm: Nature and Joy*. London: John Murray, 2015.

McCully, Patrick. *Silenced Rivers: The Ecology and Politics of Large Dams*. London: Zed Books, 1996.

McGregor, Joan. *Crossing the Zambezi*. Oxford: James Currey, 2009.

Menzies, Gavin. *1421: The Year China Discovered the World*. London: Bantam Books, 2003.

Miłosz, Czesław. 'I Sleep a Lot'. In *Collected Poems*. New York: Ecco Publishing, 1990.

Mitford Barberton, Ivan, and Vera White. *Some Frontier Families*. Cape Town: Human and Rousseau, 1968.

Mkhize, Nokulinda. 'Of Black People and Nature'. *City Press*, 10 February 2013.

Monro, Dan. *A Brief History of the Kowie and its Environs*. Port Alfred: Kowie Museum, 1985.

Moodie, Donald. *The Record, or A Series of Official Papers Relative to the Condition and Treatment of the Native Tribes of South Africa*. Cape Town: Murray and St Leger, 1888.

Morse Jones, Eric. *The Lower Albany Chronicle. Part 1, 1806–1825; Part 2, 1824–1840; Part 3, 1841–1850; Part 4, 1851–1855; Parts 5 and 6, 1856–1900*. Port Alfred: Port Alfred Historical Society, 1968.

Moss, Cynthia. *Elephant Memories: Thirteen Years in the Life of an Elephant Family*. Chicago: University of Chicago Press, 2012.

Mostert, Noël. *Frontiers: The Epic of South Africa's Creation and the Tragedy of the Xhosa People*. New York: Knopf, 1992.

Muller, Mike. 'Working Together to Manage SA's Water Better'. *Business Day*, 19 January 2012.

Mullins, Tom. 'Grahamstown's Water Supply: A Brief History, 1812 to 2008'. Grahamstown: Kowie Catchment Campaign, 2009.

Nash, Margaret. *Bailie's Party of 1820 Settlers: A Collective Experience in Emigration*. Cape Town: Balkema, 1982.

Neethling, Edith. 'Pioneer's Castle is Still Landmark'. *Talk of the Town*, 22 June 2007.

Ngũgĩ wa Thiong'o. *Decolonising the Mind: The Politics of Language in African Literature*. London: James Currey, 1986.

Novesky, Amy. *Cloth Lullaby: The Woven Life of Louise Bourgeois*. New York: Abrams Books for Young Readers, 2016.

Nsubuga, Yvonne Nakalo. 'Towards Sustainable Utilisation of the Fishery Resources of the Kowie Estuary, South Africa'. MA thesis, Rhodes University, 2014.

Oliver, Mary. *Upstream: Selected Essays*. New York: Random House, 2016.

Orthofer, Anna. 'Wealth Inequality in South Africa'. Working Paper 15, Research Project on Employment, Income Distribution and Inclusive Growth, University of Cape Town, 2016.

PACSA (Pietermaritzburg Agency for Community Social Action). 'PACSA Monthly Food Price Barometer: March 2016'. http://www.pacsa.org.za/images/food_barometer/2016/March_2016_PACSA_monthly_food_price_barometer.pdf.

Palmer, Eve. *The Plains of Camdeboo*. Johannesburg: Penguin Random House, 1996.

Paterson, Angus. 'Salt Marshes: Jewels of the Eastern Cape'. *Eastern Cape Estuaries Management Programme Newsletter* 4 (Summer 2000): 3–6.

Peires, Jeff. *The Dead Will Arise.* Johannesburg: Ravan Press, 1989.

Peires, Jeff. 'An Early History of the Zuurveld'. *The Toposcope* 51 (2010): 66–68.

Peires, Jeff. *The House of Phalo: A History of the Xhosa People in the Days of Their Independence.* Johannesburg: Ravan Press, 1981.

Peires, Jeff. 'How the Eastern Cape Lost Its Edge'. In *The Fate of the Eastern Cape: History, Politics and Social Policy*, ed. Greg Ruiters, 1–15. Pietermaritzburg: UKZN Press, 2011.

Peires, Jeff. 'The Other Side of the Black Silk Handkerchief.' *Quarterly Bulletin of the National Library of South Africa* 62 (2008): 9–33.

Penn, Nigel. ' "Close and Merciful Watchfulness": John Montagu's Convict System in the Mid-Nineteenth-Century Cape Colony'. *Cultural and Social History* 5, 4 (1980): 465–480.

Penn, Nigel. *The Forgotten Frontier.* Cape Town: Double Storey Books, 2005.

Pinnock, Don. 'Damn Dams'. watercaucus@googlegroups.com, accessed 13 May 2014.

Pinnock, Don. *The Woman Who Lived in a Tree.* Johannesburg: Jacana Media, 2009.

Pringle, Thomas. *Narrative of a Residence in South Africa.* Cape Town: Struik, 1966 [1835].

Proulx, Annie. *Bird Cloud: A Memoir of Place.* London: Fourth Estate, 2012.

'Ramhoa and Ndlambe Appeal Kowie River Record of Decisions'. *The Announcer*, 10 April 2015.

Rasa, Anna. *Mongoose Watch: A Family Observed.* London: John Murray, 1984.

Reddy, Thiven. *South Africa, Settler Colonialism and the Failures of Liberal Democracy.* Johannesburg: Wits University Press, 2016.

Rees, Penny. 'The uMngeni River'. *Environment, People and Conservation in Africa* 15 (Winter 2013): 44–47.

'Rendel's Fame Rested on Engineering Skill'. *The Toposcope* 21 (1990): 34–36.

Rivett-Carnac, Dorothy. *Thus Came the English.* Cape Town: Howard Timmins, 1961.

Rose, William. 'Personal Reminiscences from the 1870s'. In *Looking Back at Port Alfred*, edited by Douglas Bailes, 9–38. Port Alfred: Kowie History Museum, 2006.

Ross, Robert. *The Borders of Race in Colonial South Africa: The Kat River Settlement 1820–1850.* Cambridge: Cambridge University Press, 2014.

Ruiters, Greg. 'Transformative Municipal Services in the Eastern Cape'. In *The Fate of the Eastern Cape: History, Politics and Social Policy*, ed. Greg Ruiters, 219–237. Pietermaritzburg: UKZN Press, 2011.

Schreiner, Olive. *From Man to Man*, ed. Dorothy Driver. Cape Town: UCT Press, 2015 [1926].

Scott, James B., ed. *Letter Book of Sir Rufane Shaw Donkin*. Port Elizabeth: Historical Society, 1970.

Seal, Jeremy. *Meander East to West, Indirectly, along a Turkish River*. New York: Bloomsbury, 2012.

Shiva, Vandana. *Making Peace with the Earth: Beyond Resource, Land and Food Wars*. New Delhi: Women Unlimited, 2012; Johannesburg: Jacana Media, 2013.

Short, Damian. *Redefining Genocide: Settler Colonialism, Social Death and Ecocide*. London: Zed Books, 2016.

Skead, Jack. *Historical Mammal Incidence in the Cape Province*, vol. 2. Cape Town: Chief Directorate of Nature Conservation; Port Elizabeth: Nelson Mandela Metropolitan University, 2007.

Slaughter, Ronnie. 'How Port Alfred Started Drinking Kowie River Water'. Unpublished paper, n.d.

Smith, J.L.B. *The Sea Fishes of Southern Africa*. Johannesburg: Central News Agency, 1950.

Solnit, Rebecca. *The Faraway Nearby*. London: Granta, 2014.

Sparrman, Anders. *Travels in the Cape 1772–76*, vol. 2, edited by Vernon Forbes. Cape Town: Van Riebeeck Society, 1977.

Stead, Jonathan. *The Development and Failure of the Eastern Cape Separatist Movement*. Pretoria: Government Printer, 1984.

Stelli, Samantha. 'Wetlands: Essential Ecosystem That Requires Our Protection'. *Environment, People and Conservation in Africa* 12 (Spring 2012): 20–23.

Stone, Christopher D. *Should Trees Have Standing? Law, Morality and the Environment*, 3rd edn. New York: Oxford University Press, 2010.

Stretch, Charles L. *The Journal of Charles Lennox Stretch*, ed. Basil Le Cordeur. Cape Town: Maskew Miller, 1988.

Stretch, Charles. 'Makana and the Attack on Grahamstown in 1819'. *Cape Monthly Magazine* 12 (1876): 279–303.

Strydom, Nadine. 'Dynamics of Early Stage Fishes Associated with Selected Warm Temperate Estuaries in South Africa'. PhD thesis, Rhodes University, 2000.

Taylor, Stephen. *The Caliban Shore: The Fate of the Grosvenor Castaways*. London: Faber and Faber, 2004.

Theal, George M. *History of South Africa from 1795 to 1872*, 5th edn, vol. 1. London: George Allen and Unwin, 1927.

Thompson, George. *Travels and Adventures in Southern Africa*, vol. 1. London: Henry Colburn, 1827.

Thoreau, Henry. *Walking*. Boston: Beacon Press, 1991 [1863].

Thoreau, Henry. *Where I Lived and What I Lived For*. London: Penguin Books, 2005 [1854].

Tocqueville, Alexis de. *Democracy in America*. New York: Alfred A. Knopf, 1946 [1835].

Todd, Biff. *The Kowie River*. Port Alfred: Kowie Museum, n.d.

Trapido, Stanley. 'The Origins of the Cape Franchise Qualification'. *Journal of African History* 5, 1 (1964): 37–54.

Tsing, Anna. *The Mushroom at the End of the World: On the Possibility of Life in Capitalist Ruins*. Princeton: Princeton University Press, 2015.

Tucker, Eric. 'The Castle above the Kowie'. *Eastern Province Herald*, 12 August 1970.

Turpie, J.K. 'An Assessment of the Conservation Priority Status of South African Estuaries for Use in Management and Water Allocation', 190–204. Pretoria: *Water SA* 28, 2 (April 2002): 200.

Turpin, Eric. *Basket Work Harbour: The Story of the Kowie*. Cape Town: Howard Timmins, 1964.

Turpin, Eric. 'The Kowie Harbour'. *The Toposcope* 6 (1975): 40–46.

Twigger, Robert. *Red Nile*. London: Phoenix, 2014.

United Nations Environmental Programme. *The World's Water Quality*. Nairobi: UNEP, 2016.

Veracini, Lorenzo. *Settler Colonialism: A Theoretical Overview*. London: Palgrave Macmillan, 2010.

Wainwright, Hilary. *The Tragedy of the Private, the Potential of the Public*. London: Transnational Institute, Public Services International, 2014.

Wells, Julie. *Rebellion and Uproar: Makhanda and the Great Escape from Robben Island, 1820*. Pretoria: Unisa Press, 2007.

Wells, Julie. *The Return of Makhanda: Exploring the Legend*. Pietermaritzburg: UKZN Press, 2012.

Whitfield, Alan. 'Are We Looking After Our Estuaries?' *Environment, People and Conservation in Africa* 9 (2011): 8–9.

Wiener, Jonathan. *The Beak of the Finch*. London: Croom Helm, 1983.

Williams, Donovan. *When Races Meet: The Life and Times of William Ritchie Thompson*. Johannesburg: A.P.B. Publishers, 1967.

Williams, Raymond. *Keywords*. Harmondsworth: Penguin, 1980.

Winchester, Simon. *The River at the Centre of the World*. London: Picador, 1996.

WoMin. *No Longer a Life Worth Living*. Johannesburg: WoMin, 2016.

Primary and archival sources

Cape of Good Hope Colony, Colonial Office Papers, Western Cape Archives, CA CO 6267 (Letters and reports received on Convict Stations), CA CO 6287

(Letters and reports received on Kowie Convict Station, 1864), CA CO 6272 (Letters and reports received from Convict Stations Grahamstown and Kowie, 1861), CA CO 6262 (Letters and reports received from Convict Stations Grahamstown, Kowie, Port Elizabeth), CA CO 6278 (Letters and reports received from Convict Stations Grahamstown, Kowie, Katberg, Paarde-Poort, 1862).

Cock, Letitia Harriet. 'Reminiscences of Richmond Villa, Kimberley [1946]'. MS 14247, Cory Library, Rhodes University.

Cock, William. Journal. MS 14262, Cory Library, Rhodes University.

Cock, William. Letters. MS 14263, Cory Library, Rhodes University.

Godlonton, Robert. Journal of 30 August–October 1850. A655, Historical Papers, University of the Witwatersrand.

Godlonton, Robert. Letters 1830–1884. A43, Historical Papers, Wits University.

Reports

Afri-Coast Engineers. *Draft Environmental Management Programme: Dredging of the Kowie Estuary and the Royal Alfred Marina Canals and the Disposal of Dredged Spoil*. Submitted to DEDEAT, 2014.

Afri-Coast Engineers. *Dredging of the Royal Alfred Marina Canals and the Disposal of Dredge Spoil*. Final Basic Assessment Report Submitted to Department of Development, Environment and Tourism (DEDEAT), 21 May 2014, Ref P5539001.

Allanson, Chris. *Environmental Impact Assessment Phase 1 Baseline Data Report* (undated).

Cowley, Paul, and Craig Daniel. *Review of Estuaries in the Ndlambe Coastal Region*. Report no. 229. Pietermaritzburg: Institute of Natural Resources, 2001.

Department of Development, Environment and Tourism. *Environmental Authorisation for Dredging of the Marina Canals*. Pretoria: Government Printer, 2015.

Department of Development, Environment and Tourism. *White Paper on Sustainable Coastal Development*. Pretoria: Government Printer, 2000.

Department of Environmental Affairs. *National Climate Change Response Green Paper*. Pretoria: Government Printer, 2010.

Gleneagles Environmental Consulting. *Environmental Impact Assessment: Draft Scoping Report on the Dredging of the Royal Alfred Marina and Lower Reaches of the Kowie Estuary and Disposal of Soil*, March 2005.

Gleneagles Environmental Consulting. *Environmental Impact Assessment: Scoping Report on the Dredging of the Royal Port Alfred Marina and Lower Reaches of the Kowie Estuary and Disposal of Soil*, April 2005.

Ndlambe Municipality. *Annual Report 2012/2013*.

Ndlambe Municipality. 'Dredging of Lower Reaches of Kowie River', appeal 30.6.2015 against the refusal notice.

Ndlambe Municipality. 'Integrated Development Plan 2012–2017: Draft Review 2016–2017', 2016.

Ndlambe Municipality. 'Ndlambe Municipality Section 72: Mid-Year Budget and Performance Report: 2015/2016', 2016.

Plan Associates. 'Port Alfred Environmental Impact Assessment: Phase 2, Marina and Small Craft Harbour Impacts', 1986.

Shepstone and Wylie Attorneys. 'Appeal Lodged in Terms of Regulation 61 of the 2010 EIA Regulations and Section 43 of the National Environmental Management Act 107 of 1998 on Behalf of Royal Alfred Marina Home Owners Association against the Decision of the Eastern Cape Department of Economic Development, Environmental Affairs and Tourism for: Dredging of the Lower Reaches of the Kowie River Estuary adjacent to the Royal Alfred Marina, Port Alfred within the Ndlambe Municipality'. Reference EC05/C/LN1/18/32-2013.

Shepstone and Wylie Attorneys. 'Appellants' answering statement to Keryn van der Walt in terms of Regulation 63(2)(b)', 2015.

Statistics South Africa. 'Census 2011 Municipal Report: Eastern Cape', Pretoria, 2012.

Statistics South Africa. 'General Household Survey Data 2002–2014', Pretoria, 2014.

Statistics South Africa. 'General Household Survey 2015', Pretoria, 2015.

Statistics South Africa. 'General Household Survey Series Volume 7: Housing from a Human Settlement Perspective', Pretoria, 2016.

Index

The word '*Plate*' indicates artworks and photographs.

Whanganui River 139–140
white milkwoods *see* milkwood trees
White Steenbras 23, 113
Whitfield, Alan 23, 131
Williams, Raymond 137
Willshire, Colonel 53, 55, 59
Wilmot, Keith 103
Winchester, Simon 7
WoMin 137
Wood, Aidan 116
Wood, George 96

X
Xhosa cosmology 16, 55
Xhosa people
  armed clashes with Dutch 3, 39–41
  attacks on Khoikhoi 38
  British annexation of territory 94–95
  cultural/spiritual value
    in nature 20–21
  diviner-healers 3–4, 16–18, 19,
    Plate 3
  'ecologically induced genocide' 127
  encounters with settlers 74
  forced into wage labour 87, 90, 128
  intermarried with Khoikhoi 37, 38
  modern-day poverty 13, 124, 127
  river rituals 20
  sacred qualities of rivers 3, 15, 16–17
  tactical strengths in battle
    for Zuurveld 70
  trade with Europeans 43, 84, 90, 91

various descriptions of 45, 46, 48
Xhosa prisoners 87
Zuurveld, expulsion from 40,
  58–59, 60–65, 127
Zuurveld, inhabitants of 3, 38–39, 74
see also Battle of Grahamstown

Y
Yamuna River 139
yellowwood trees 3, 8, 27, 46

Z
zostera beds 32
Zuurveld
  animal species 29, 46
  Barrow's description of 46
  boundaries of 1
  British expulsion of the Xhosa
    40, 58–59, 60–65, 127
  conflict about access to
    land/water 69, 70
  defined as Kowie catchment area 36
  Dutch–Khoikhoi clashes 3, 37–38
  Dutch–Xhosa clashes 3, 39–41
  inhabited by Khoikhoi 2, 37, 74
  inhabited by Xhosa 3, 38–39, 74
  now known as Ndlambe
    Municipal Area 2
  renamed Albany 58, 71
  suitability as pasture 36
  Thompson's description of 48
Zwartkops River 39, 45

Printed and bound by CPI Group (UK) Ltd, Croydon, CR0 4YY

09/06/2025

14685804-0002